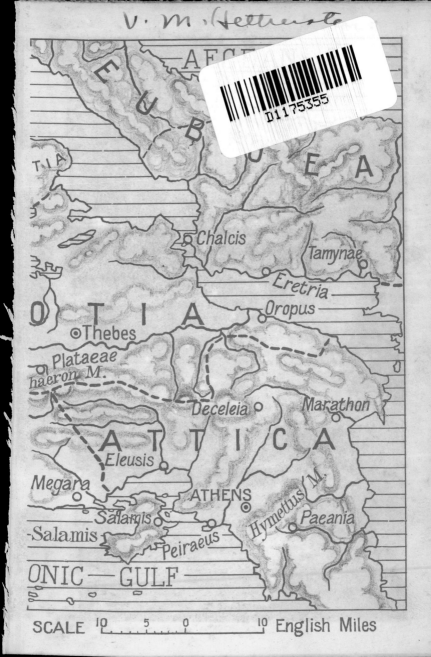

v. m. Hettrust

SCALE 10 . . . . 5 . . . . 0 . . . . . 10 English Miles

HENRY FROWDE, M.A.
PUBLISHER TO THE UNIVERSITY OF OXFORD
LONDON, EDINBURGH, NEW YORK
TORONTO AND MELBOURNE

30048

ON THE CHERSONESE (Or. VIII)

[*Introduction.* Late in the year 343 (some time after the acquittal of Aeschines) Philip invaded Epirus, made Alexander, brother of his wife Olympias, king of the Molossi instead of Arybbas, and so secured his own influence in that region. Arybbas was honourably received at Athens. Philip next threatened Ambracia and Leucas, which were colonies of Corinth, and promised to restore Naupactus, which was in the hands of the Achaeans, to the Aetolians. But Athens sent Demosthenes, Hegesippus, Polyeuctus and others to rouse the Corinthians to resistance, and also dispatched a force of citizens to Acarnania to help in the defence against Philip. Philip thereupon returned, captured Echinus and Nicaea on the Malian Gulf, and established a tetrarch in each division of Thessaly (343 B.C., or early in 342). In 342 Philistides was established, by Philip's influence, as tyrant at Oreus in Euboea (as Cleitarchus had been at Eretria in the preceding year), and the democratic leader Euphraeus committed suicide in prison.[1] The town of Chalcis, however, under Callias and Taurosthenes, remained friendly to Athens, and made a treaty of alliance with her.

About the same time a controversy, begun in the previous year, in regard to Halonnesus, was renewed. This island had belonged to Athens, but had been occupied by pirates. At some time not recorded (but probably since the Peace of 346) Philip had expelled the pirates and taken possession of the island. He now sent a letter, offering to *give* Halonnesus to Athens, but not to *give it back* (since this would concede their right to it) ; or else to submit the dispute to arbitration. He also offered to discuss a treaty for the settlement of private disputes between Athenians and Macedonians,

---

[1] See Third Philippic §§ 59 sqq.

and to concert measures with Athens for clearing the Aegean of pirates. He was willing to extend the advantages of the Peace to other Greek States, but not to agree that he and Athens should respectively possess ' what was their own ', instead of ' what they held ' ; though he was ready to submit to arbitration in regard to Cardia and other disputed places. He again denied having made the promises attributed to him, and asked for the punishment of those who slandered him. Hegesippus replied in an extant speech (' On Halonnesus '), while Demosthenes insisted that no impartial arbitrator could possibly be found. Philip's terms in regard to Halonnesus were refused, but the Athenian claim to the island was not withdrawn.

Philip spent the greater part of 342 and 341 in Thrace, mainly in the valley of the Hebrus, where he endured very great hardships through the winter, and founded colonies of Macedonian soldiers, the chief of these being Philippopolis and Cabyle. He also entered into relations with the Getae, beyond the Haemus, and garrisoned Apollonia on the Euxine. These operations were all preparatory to his projected attack upon Byzantium. (Byzantium and Athens were at this time on unfriendly terms, owing to the part taken by the latter in the Social War.)

But the immediate subject of the present Speech was the state of affairs in the Chersonese in 342. The Chersonese (with the exception of Cardia) had been secured for Athens in 357, but had been threatened by Philip in 352,[1] when he made alliance with Cardia, and forced the neighbouring Thracian Prince Cersobleptes to submit. Soon after the Peace of Philocrates, Athens sent settlers to the Chersonese under Diopeithes. Cardia alone refused to receive them, and Diopeithes, with a mercenary force, prepared to compel the Cardians to admit them; while Philip sent troops to hold the town, and complained to Athens in threatening terms of the actions of Diopeithes, and more particularly of an inroad which Diopeithes had made upon Philip's territory

[1] See Introduction to First Philippic.

in Thrace.   Diopeithes had been ill-supported with money
and men by Athens, and had had recourse to piratical actions,
in order to obtain supplies, thus arousing some indignation
at Athens ; but the prospect of the heavy expenditure
which would be necessary, if an expedition were sent to his
aid, was also unattractive.   Demosthenes, however, proposed
that Diopeithes should be vigorously supported, on the
ground that Philip was really at war with Athens, and that
this was not the time to interfere with the general who alone
was pushing the Athenian cause.   The speech was delivered
early in the spring of 341.   It is a masterpiece of oratory,
at once statesmanlike and impassioned, and shows a complete
command of every variety of tone.   The latter part of it
contains a strong denunciation of the Macedonian party in
Athens, a defence of the orator's own career, and an urgent
demand for the punishment of disloyalty.   At the same time
Demosthenes does not embody the policy which he advises
in any formal motion.   For this we have to wait for the Third
Philippic.]

It was the duty, men of Athens, of every speaker not to 1
allow either malice or favour to influence any speech which
he might make, but simply to declare the policy which he
considered to be the best, particularly when your deliberations
were concerned with public affairs of great importance.   But
since there are some who are led on to address you, partly
out of contentiousness, partly from causes which I need not
discuss, it is for you, men of Athens—you, the People—to dismiss all other considerations, and both in the votes that you
give and in the measures that you take to attend solely to
what you believe to be for the good of the city.   Now our 2
present anxiety arises out of affairs in the Chersonese, and the
campaign, now in its eleventh month, which Philip is con-
ducting in Thrace.   But most of the speeches which we have

heard have been about the acts and intentions of Diopeithes. For my part, I conceive that all charges made against any one who is amenable to the laws and can be punished by you when you will are matters which you are free to investigate, either immediately or after an interval, as you think fit; and there is no occasion for me or any one else to use strong 3 language about them. But all those advantages which an actual enemy of the city, with a large force in the Hellespont, is trying to snatch from you, and which, if we once fall behind-hand, we shall no longer be able to recover—these, surely, are matters upon which our interest demands that our plans be formed and our preparations made with the utmost dispatch; and that no clamour, no accusations about other matters, be allowed to drive us from this point.

4   Often as I am surprised at the assertions which are habitually made in your presence, nothing, men of Athens, has surprised me more than the remark which I heard only lately in the Council—that one who advises you ought, forsooth, to advise 5 you plainly either to go to war or to keep the peace. Very good.[1] If Philip is remaining inactive, if he is keeping nothing that is ours, in violation of the Peace, if he is not organizing all mankind against us, there is nothing more to be said—we have simply to observe the Peace; and I see that, for your part, you are quite ready to do so. But what if the oath that we swore, and the terms upon which we made the Peace, 6 stand inscribed for our eyes to see? What if it is proved that from the outset, before Diopeithes sailed from Athens with the settlers who are now accused of having brought about the war, Philip wrongfully seized many of our possessions—and here, unrepealed, are your resolutions charging him with

[1] ἔστω δή.

this—and that all along he has been uninterruptedly seizing
the possessions of the other Hellenic and foreign peoples,
and uniting their resources against us? What is *then* the
meaning of the statement that we ought either to go to war
or to keep the Peace? For we have no choice in the matter : 7
nothing remains open to us but the most righteous and most
necessary of all acts—the act that they deliberately refuse to
consider—I mean the act of retaliation against the aggressor :
unless indeed, they intend to argue that, so long as Philip
keeps away from Attica and the Peiraeus, he does the city no
wrong and is not committing acts of war. But if *this* is their 8
criterion of right and wrong, if *this* is their definition of peace,
then, although what they say is iniquitous, intolerable, and
inconsistent with your security, as all must see, at the same
time these very statements are actually contradictory of the
charges which they are making against Diopeithes. Why, 9
I beg to ask,[n] are we to give Philip full leave to act in whatever
way he chooses, so long as he does not touch Attica, when
Diopeithes is not to be allowed even to assist the Thracians,
without being accused of initiating war? But even if this
inconsistency is brought home to them, still, we are told, the
conduct of the mercenaries in ravaging the Hellespontine
country is outrageous, and Diopeithes has no right to drive
the vessels to shore,[n] and ought to be stopped. I grant it : 10
let it be done : I have nothing to say against it. Yet nevertheless, if their advice is genuinely based on considerations
of right, and right alone, I consider that they are bound
to prove that, as surely as they are seeking to break up the
force on which *Athens* at present relies, by slandering its
commander to you when he tries to provide funds to support
it, so surely *Philip's* force will be disbanded if you accept

their advice. If they fail to prove this, you must consider that they are simply setting the city once more upon the same course which has already resulted in the utter ruin
11 of her fortunes. For surely you know that nothing in the world has contributed so much to Philip's successes, as his being always first on the scene of action. With a standing force always about him, and knowing beforehand what he intends to do, he suddenly falls upon whomsoever he pleases : while we wait until we learn that something is happening,
12 and only then, in a turmoil, make our preparations. It follows, of course, that every position which he has attacked, he holds in undisturbed possession ; while we are all behind-hand ; all our expenditure proves to have been so much useless waste ; we have displayed our hostility and our desire to check him ; but we are too late for action, and so we add disgrace to failure.

13　　You must therefore not fail to recognize, men of Athens, that now, as before, all else that you hear consists of mere words and pretexts ; and that the real aim of all that is being done is to secure that you may remain at home, that Athens may have no force outside the city, and that thus Philip may give effect to all his desires without let or hindrance. Consider, in the first place, what is actually occurring at
14 the present moment. He is at present passing the time [n] in Thrace, with a great army under him ; and, as we are told by those who are on the spot,[n] he is sending for a large addition to it from Macedonia and Thessaly. Now if he waits for the Etesian winds,[n] and then goes to Byzantium and besieges it, tell me first whether you think that the Byzantines will persist in their present infatuation,[n] and will not
15 call upon you and entreat you to go to their aid ? I do not

think so. Why, I believe that they would open their gates
to men whom they distrust even more than they distrust
you (if such exist), rather than surrender the city to Philip—
supposing, that is, that he does not capture them first. And
then, if we are unable to set sail from Athens, and if there are
no forces there on the spot to help them, nothing can prevent
their destruction. 'Of course,' you say, 'for the men are 16
possessed, and their infatuation passes all bounds.' Very
true; and yet they must be preserved; for the interests of
Athens require it. And besides, we cannot by any means
be certain that he will not invade the Chersonese. Indeed,
if we are to judge by the letter which he has sent to you, he
there says that he *will* punish the settlers [n] in the Chersonese.
If then the army that is now formed there is in existence, it 17
will be able to help the Chersonese, and to injure some part
of Philip's country. But when once it is dissolved, what
shall we do if he marches against the Chersonese? 'We shall
of course put Diopeithes on his trial.' And how will that
improve our position? 'Well, we should go to the rescue
from Athens ourselves.' What if the winds make it impossible?
'But, of course, he will not really get there.' And who can 18
guarantee that? Do you realize, men of Athens, or take into
account, what the coming season of the year is, the season
against which some think you ought to evacuate the Hellespont and hand it over to Philip? What if, when he leaves
Thrace, he does not go near the Chersonese or Byzantium
at all—for this, too, is a possibility which you must consider—
but comes to Chalcis [n] or Megara, just as he lately came to
Oreus? Is it better to resist him here, and to allow the war
to come into Attica, or to provide something to keep him
busy there? The latter course is surely the better.

19 Realizing these things, therefore, as you all must, and taking due account of them, you must not, Heaven knows, look askance at the force which Diopeithes is trying to provide for Athens, or attempt to disband it. You must yourselves prepare another force to support it: you must help him freely with money, and give him in all other respects your

20 loyal co-operation. If Philip were asked to say whether he would wish these soldiers who are now with Diopeithes—describe them as you will, for I in no way dispute your description—to be prosperous and in high favour with the Athenians, and to be augmented in numbers by the co-operation of the city; or whether he would rather see them broken up and destroyed in consequence of calumnious charges against them; he would prefer, I imagine, the latter alternative. Can it then be, that there are men among us here who are trying to bring about the very thing that Philip would pray Heaven for? And if so, do you need to seek any further for the cause of the total ruin of the city's fortunes?

21 I wish, therefore, to examine without reserve the present crisis of our affairs, to inquire what we ourselves are now doing, and how we are dealing with it. We do not wish to contribute funds, nor to serve with the forces in person; we cannot keep our hands from the public revenues; [n] we do not give the contributions of the allies [n] to Diopeithes, nor do we

22 approve of such supplies as he raises for himself; but we look malignantly at him, we ask whence he gets them, what he intends to do, and every possible question of that kind: and yet we are still not willing to confine ourselves to our own affairs, in consequence of the attitude which we have adopted; we still praise with our lips those who uphold the dignity of the city, though in our acts we are fighting on the side of their

opponents. Now whenever any one rises to speak, you always 23
put to him the question ' What are we to do ? ' I wish to put
to *you* the question, ' What are we to *say* ? ' For if you will
neither contribute, nor serve in person, nor leave the public
funds alone, nor grant him the contributions, nor let him
get what he can for himself, nor yet confine yourselves to
your own affairs, I do not know what I can say. For when you
give such licence to those who desire to make charges and
accusations, that you listen to them even when they denounce
him by anticipation for his alleged intentions—well, what
can one say ?

The possible effect of this is a matter which some of you 24
require to understand, and I will speak without reserve ;
for indeed I could not speak otherwise. All the commanders
who have ever yet sailed from Athens—if I am wrong, I
consent to any penalty that you please [n]—take money from the
Chians, from the Erythraeans,[n] from any people from whom
they can severally get it—I mean, any of the Asiatic settlers
who are now in question. Those who have one or two ships 25
take less, those who have a larger force take more. And those
who give to them do not give either little or much for
nothing ; they are not so insane : in fact, with these sums
they buy immunity from injury for the merchants who sail
from their ports, freedom from piracy, the convoying of
their vessels, and so on. They call the gifts ' benevolences ',[n]
and that is the name given to the sums thus obtained. And 26
in the present case, when Diopeithes is there with his army,
it is obvious that all these peoples will give him money.
From what other source do you imagine that a general can
maintain his troops, when he has received nothing from you,
and has no resources from which he can pay his men ? Will

money drop from the sky? Of course not. He subsists upon
27 what he can collect or beg or borrow. The real effect, therefore, of the accusations made against him here, is simply to warn
every one that they should refuse to give him anything, since
he is to pay the penalty for his very intentions, not to speak of
any action that he may have taken or any success that he may
have achieved. That is the only meaning of the cry that 'he
is preparing a blockade', or 'he is surrendering [n] the Hellenes'. Do any of his critics care about the Hellenes who
28 live in Asia? Were it so, they would be more thoughtful for
the rest of mankind than for their own country. And the proposal to send another general to the Hellespont amounts to
no more than this. For if Diopeithes is acting outrageously
and is driving the vessels to shore, then, gentlemen, one
little wax-tablet [n] is enough to put an end to it all: and what
the laws command is that for these offences we should im-
peach the wrong-doers—not that we should keep a watch upon
29 our own forces at such expense and with so many ships.[n] Such
insanity really passes all bounds. No! Against the enemy
whom we cannot arrest and render amenable to the laws,
it is both right and necessary to maintain a force, to send
war-ships, and to contribute war-funds: but against one of
ourselves, a decree, an impeachment, a dispatch-boat [n] will
answer our purpose. These are the means which sensible
men would use: the policy of the other side is the policy
30 of men whose spitefulness [n] is ruining your fortunes. And
that there should be some such men, bad though it is, is not
the worst. No! for you who sit there are already in such
a frame of mind, that if any one comes forward and says that
Diopeithes is the cause of all the mischief, or Chares,[n] or
Aristophon,[n] or any Athenian citizen that he happens to

name, you at once agree, and clamorously declare that he
is right; but if any one comes forward and tells you the 31
truth, and says, 'Men of Athens, this is nonsense. It is
Philip that is the cause of all this mischief and trouble; for
if he were quiet, the city would have nothing to disturb
her,' you cannot, indeed, deny the truth of his words, but
you seem, I think, to be annoyed, as though you were losing
something.[n] And the cause of these things is this—and 32
I beseech you, in Heaven's name, to let me speak unreservedly,
when I am speaking for your true good—that some of your
politicians have contrived that you should be terrifying and
severe in your assemblies, but easy-going and contemptible
in your preparations for war. And accordingly, if any one
names as the culprit some one whom you know you can arrest
in your own midst, you agree and you wish to act; but if
one is named whom you must first master by force of arms,
if you are to punish him at all, you are at a loss, I fancy,
what to do, and you are vexed when this is brought home to
you. For your politicians, men of Athens, should have 33
treated you in exactly the opposite way to this; they should
train you to be kind and sympathetic in your assemblies; for
there it is with the members of your own body and your own
allies that your case is argued: but your terrors and your
severity should be displayed in your preparations for war,
where the struggle is with your enemies and your rivals.
As it is, by their popular speeches, and by courting your 34
favour to excess, they have brought you into such a condition that, while in your assemblies you give yourselves
airs and enjoy their flattery, listening to nothing but what
is meant to please you, in the world of facts and
events you are in the last extremity of peril. Imagine, in

God's name, what would happen, if the Hellenes were to
call you to account for the opportunities which, in your
indolence, you have now let pass, and were to put to you the
35 question, ' Is it true, men of Athens, that you send envoys
to us on every possible occasion, to tell us of Philip's designs
against ourselves and all the Hellenes, and of the duty of
keeping guard against the man, and to warn us in every
way ? ' We should have to confess that it was true. We
do act thus. ' Then,' they would proceed, ' is it true, you
most contemptible of all men, that though the man has been
36 away for ten months, and has been cut off from every
possibility of returning home, by illness and by winter and by
wars, you have neither liberated Euboea nor recovered any of
your own possessions ? Is it true that you have remained at
home, unoccupied and healthy—if such a word can be used
of men who behave thus—and have seen him set up two
tyrants in Euboea, one to serve as a fortress directly menacing
37 Attica, the other to watch Sciathus ; and that you have not
even rid yourselves of these dangers—granted that you
did not want to do anything more—but have let them be ?
Obviously you have retired in his favour, and have made it
evident that if he dies ten times over, you will not make
any move the more. Why trouble us then with your embassies and your accusations ? ' If they speak thus to us,
what will be our answer ? What shall we say, Athenians ?
I do not see what we can say.

38 Now there are some who imagine that they confute a
speaker, as soon as they have asked him the question, ' What
then are we to do ? ' I will first give them this answer—the
most just and true of all—' Do not do what you are doing
39 now.' But at the same time I will give them a minute and

detailed reply ; and then let them show that their willingness
to act upon it is not less than their eagerness to interrogate.
First, men of Athens, you must thoroughly make up your
minds to the fact that Philip is at war with Athens, and has
broken the Peace—you must cease to lay the blame at one
another's doors—and that he is evilly-disposed and hostile
to the whole city, down to the very ground on which it is
built ; nay, I will go further—hostile to every single man 40
in the city, even to those who are most sure that they are
winning his favour. (If you think otherwise, consider the
case of Euthycrates [n] and Lasthenes of Olynthus, who fancied
that they were on the most friendly terms with him, but,
after they had betrayed their city, suffered the most utter
ruin of all.) But his hostilities and intrigues are aimed at
nothing so much as at our constitution, whose overthrow
is the very first object in the world to him. And in a sense 41
it is natural that he should aim at this. For he knows very
well that even if he becomes master of all the rest of the world,
he can retain nothing securely, so long as you are a democracy ;
and that if he chances to stumble anywhere, as may often
happen to a man, all the elements which are now forced into
union with him will come and take refuge with you. For 42
though you are not yourselves naturally adapted for aggrand-
izement or the usurpation of empire, you have the art of
preventing any other from seizing power and of taking it
from him when he has it ; and in every respect you are ready
to give trouble to those who are ambitious of dominion, and
to lead all men forth into liberty. And so he would not
have Freedom, from her home in Athens, watching for every
opportunity he may offer—far from it—and there is nothing
unsound or careless in his reasoning. The first essential 43

point, therefore, is this—that you conceive him to be the irreconcilable foe of your constitution and of democracy : for unless you are inwardly convinced of this, you will not be willing to take an active interest in the situation. Secondly, you must realize clearly that all the plans which he is now so busily contriving are in the nature of preparations against this country ; and wherever any one resists him, he there

44 resists him on our behalf. For surely no one is so simple as to imagine that when Philip is covetous of the wretched hamlets [n] of Thrace—one can give no other name to Drongilum, Cabyle, Masteira, and the places which he is now seizing— and when to get these places he is enduring heavy labours,

45 hard winters, and the extremity of danger ;—no one can imagine, I say, that the harbours and the dockyards, and the ships of the Athenians, the produce of your silver-mines, and your huge revenue, have no attraction for him, or that he will leave you in possession of these, while he winters in the very pit of destruction [n] for the sake of the millet and the spelt in the silos [n] of Thrace. No, indeed ! It is to get these into his power that he pursues both his operations in Thrace

46 and all his other designs. What then, as sensible men, must you do ? Knowing and realizing your position, as you do, you must lay aside this excessive, this irremediable [n] indolence : you must contribute funds, and require them from your allies ; you must so provide and act, that this force which is now assembled may be held together ; in order that, as Philip has the force in readiness that is to injure and enslave all the Hellenes, you may have in readiness that which shall

47 preserve and succour them. You cannot effect by isolated expeditions any of the things which must be effected. You *must* organize a force, and provide maintenance for it, and

paymasters, and a staff of servants ; and when you have taken such steps as will ensure the strictest possible watch being kept over the funds, you must hold these officials accountable for the money, and the general for the actual operations. If you act thus, and honestly make up your minds to take this course, you will either compel Philip to observe a righteous peace and remain in his own land—and no greater blessing could you obtain than that—or you will fight him on equal terms.

It may be thought that this policy demands heavy expendi- 48 ture, and great exertions and trouble. That is true indeed ; but let the objector take into account what the consequences to the city must be, if he is unwilling to assent to this policy, and he will find that the ready performance of duty brings its reward. If indeed some god is offering us his guarantee— 49 for no human guarantee would be sufficient in so great a matter—that if you remain at peace and let everything slide, Philip will not in the end come and attack yourselves ; then, although, before God and every Heavenly Power, it would be unworthy of you and of the position that the city holds, and of the deeds of our forefathers, to abandon all the rest of the Hellenes to slavery for the sake of our own ease —although, for my part, I would rather have died than have suggested such a thing—yet, if another proposes it and convinces you, let it be so : do not defend yourselves : let everything go. But if no one entertains such a belief, if we 50 all know that the very opposite is true, and that the wider the mastery we allow him to gain, the more difficult and powerful a foe we shall have to deal with, what further subterfuge is open to us ? Why do we delay ? When shall 51 we ever be willing, men of Athens, to do our duty ? 'When

B

we are compelled,' you say. But the hour of compulsion, as the word is applied to free men, is not only here already, but has long passed ; and we must surely pray that the compulsion which is put upon slaves may not come upon us. And what is the difference ? It is this—that for a free man the greatest compelling force is his shame at the course which events are taking—I do not know what greater we can imagine ; but the slave is compelled by blows and bodily tortures, which I pray may never fall to our lot ; it is not fit to speak of them.

52   I would gladly tell you the whole story, and show how certain persons are working for your ruin by their policy. I pass over, however, every point but this. Whenever any question of our relations with Philip arises, at once some one stands up and talks of the blessings of peace, of the difficulty of maintaining a large force, and of designs on the part of certain persons to plunder our funds ; with other tales of the same kind, which enable them to delay your action, and give Philip time 53 to do what he wishes unopposed. What is the result ? For you the result is your leisure, and a respite from immediate action —advantages which I fear you will some day feel to have cost you dear ; and for them it is the favour they win, and the wages for these services. But I am sure that there is no need to persuade you to keep the Peace—you sit here fully persuaded. It is the man who is committing acts of war that we need to persuade ; for if he is persuaded, you are ready 54 enough. Nor is it the expenditure which is to ensure our preservation that ought to distress us, but the fate which is in prospect for us, if we are not willing to take this action : while the threatened ' plunder of our funds ' is to be prevented by the proposal of some safeguard which will render them

secure, not by the abandonment of our interests. And even 55 so, men of Athens, I feel indignant at the very fact that some of you are so much pained at the prospect of the plunder of our funds, when you have it in your power both to protect them and to punish the culprits, and yet feel no pain when Philip is seizing all Hellas piecemeal for his plunder, and seizing it to strengthen himself against you. What then is the reason, 56 men of Athens, that though Philip's campaigns, his aggressions, his seizure of cities, are so unconcealed, none of my opponents has ever said that *he* was bringing about war ? Why is it those who advise you not to allow it, not to make these sacrifices, that they accuse, and say that *they* will be the cause of the war ? I will inform you. It is because n 57 they wish to divert the anger which you are likely to show, if you suffer at all from the war, on to the heads of those who are giving you the best advice in your own interests. They want you to sit and try such persons, instead of resisting Philip ; and they themselves are to be the prosecutors, instead of paying the penalty for their present actions. That is the meaning of their assertion that there are some here, forsooth, who want to bring about war. That is the real 58 point of these allegations of responsibility. But this I know beyond all doubt—that without waiting for any one in Athens to propose the declaration of war, Philip has not only taken many other possessions of ours, but has just now sent an expedition to Cardia. If, in spite of this, we wish to pretend that he is not making war on us, he would be the most senseless man living, were he to attempt to convince us of our error. But what shall we say, when his attack is made 59 directly upon ourselves ? He of course will say that he is not at war with us—just as he was not at war with Oreus, n when his soldiers were in the land ; nor with the Pheraeans,[n] before that, when he was assaulting their walls ; nor with the Olynthians, first of all, until he and his army were actually within their territory.   Or shall we still say that those who urge resistance are bringing about war ? If so, all that is left to us is slavery. If we may neither offer resistance, nor yet be suffered to remain at peace, no other compromise [n] is possible.

60 And further, the issues at stake are not for you merely what they are for other states. What Philip desires is not your subjection, but your utter annihilation. For he knows full well that you will never consent to be his slaves, and that even if you were willing, you would not know the way, accustomed as you are to govern ; and he knows that you will be able to give him more trouble, if you get the oppor-

61 tunity, than all the rest of the world. The struggle, then, is a struggle for existence ; and as such you ought to think of it : and you should show your abhorrence of those who have sold themselves to Philip by beating them to death. For it is impossible, utterly impossible, to master your enemies outside the city, before you punish your enemies in the city itself.

62 Whence comes it, think you, that he is insulting us now (for his conduct seems to me to be nothing less than this), and that while he at least deceives all other peoples by doing them favours, he is using threats against you without more ado ? For instance, he enticed the Thessalians by large gifts into their present servitude ; and words cannot describe how greatly he deceived the Olynthians at first by the gift

63 of Poteidaea and much beside.   At this moment he is alluring the Thebans, by delivering up Boeotia to them, and ridding them of a long and arduous campaign. Each of these peoples has first reaped some advantage, before falling into those

calamities which some of them have already suffered, as all
the world knows, and some are destined to suffer whenever
their time comes. But as for yourselves, to pass over all that
you have been robbed of at an earlier period,[n] what deception,
what robbery have been practised upon you in the very act
of making the Peace! Have not the Phocians, and Ther- 64
mopylae, and the Thracian seaboard—Doriscus, Serrhium,
Cersobleptes himself—been taken from you? Does not
Philip at this moment occupy the city of the Cardians, and
avow it openly? Why is it then, that he behaves as he does
to all others, and so differently to you? Because yours is
the one city in the world where men are permitted to speak
on behalf of the enemy without fear; because here a man
may take bribes, and still address you with impunity, even
when you have been robbed of your own. In Olynthus
it was only safe to take Philip's side when the people of
Olynthus as a whole had shared Philip's favours, and was
enjoying the possession of Poteidaea. In Thessaly it was 65
only safe to take Philip's side when the Thessalian commons
had shared Philip's favours; for he had expelled the tyrants
for them, and restored to them their Amphictyonic position.
In Thebes it was not safe, until he had restored Boeotia to
Thebes and annihilated the Phocians. But at Athens— 66
though Philip has not only robbed you of Amphipolis and the
territory of the Cardians, but has turned Euboea into a
fortress overlooking your country, and is now on his way
to attack Byzantium—at Athens it *is* safe to speak in Philip's
interest. Aye, and you know that, of such speakers, some
who were poor are rapidly growing rich; and some who were
without name or fame are becoming famous and distinguished,
while you, on the other hand, are becoming inglorious

instead of famous, bankrupt instead of wealthy. For a city's wealth consists, I imagine, in allies, confidence, loyalty—
67 and of all these you are bankrupt. And because you are indifferent to these advantages, and let them drift away from you, he has become prosperous and powerful, and formidable to all, Hellenes and foreigners alike ; while you are deserted and humbled, with a splendid profusion of commodities in your market, and a contemptible lack of all those things with which you should have been provided. But I observe that certain speakers do not follow the same principles in the advice which they give you, as they follow for themselves. *You*, they tell you, ought to remain quiet, even when you are wronged ; but *they* cannot remain quiet in your presence, even when no one is wronging them.

68   But now some one or other comes forward and says, ' Ah, but you will not move a motion or take any risk. You are a poor-spirited coward.' Bold, offensive, shameless, I am not, and I trust I may never be ; and yet I think I have more courage than very many of
69 your dashing statesmen. For one, men of Athens, who overlooks all that the city's interest demands—who prosecutes, confiscates, gives, accuses—does so not from any bravery, but because in the popular character of his speeches and public actions he has a guarantee of his personal safety, and therefore is bold without risk. But one who in acting for the best sets himself in many ways against your wishes—who never speaks to please, but always to advise what is best ; one who chooses a policy in which more issues must be decided by chance than by calculation, and yet makes himself responsible to you for both—that is
70 the courageous man, and such is the citizen who is of value

to his country, rather than those who, to gain an ephemeral
popularity, have ruined the supreme interests of the city.
So far am I from envying these men, or thinking them worthy
citizens of their country, that if any one were to ask me to
say, what good *I* had really done to the city, although, men of
Athens, I could tell how often I had been trierarch and
choregus,[n] how I had contributed funds, ransomed prisoners,
and done other like acts of generosity, I would mention
none of these things ; I would say only that my policy is not 71
one of measures like theirs—that although, like others, I could
make accusations and shower favours and confiscate property
and do all that my opponents do, I have never to this day
set myself to do any of these things ; I have been influenced
neither by gain nor by ambition ; but I continue to give
the advice which sets me below many others in your estima-
tion, but which must make you greater, if you will listen to
it ; for so much, perhaps, I may say without offence. Nor, 72
I think, should I be acting fairly as a citizen, if I devised
such political measures as would at once make me the first man
in Athens, and you the last of all peoples. As the measures
of a loyal politician develop, the greatness of his country
should develop with them ; and it is the thing which is
best, not the thing which is easiest, that every speaker should
advocate. Nature will find the way to the easiest course
unaided. To the best, the words and the guidance of the
loyal citizen must show the way.

I have heard it remarked before now, that though what 73
I *say* is always what is best, still I never contribute anything
but words ; whereas the city needs work of some practical
kind. I will tell you without any concealment my own
sentiments on this matter. There *is* no work that can be

demanded of any of your public advisers, except that he
should advise what is best; and I think I can easily show
74 you that this is so. No doubt you know how the great
Timotheus [n] delivered a speech to the effect that you ought
to go to the rescue and save the Euboeans, when the Thebans
were trying to reduce them to servitude ; and how, in the
course of his speech, he spoke somewhat in this strain :—
' What ? ' said he, ' when you actually have the Thebans
in the island, do you debate what you are to do with them,
and how you are to act ? Will you not cover the sea with
warships, men of Athens ? Will you not rise from your seats
and go instantly to the Peiraeus and launch your vessels ? '
75 So Timotheus spoke, and you acted as he bade you ; and
through his speech and your action the work was done
But if he had given you the best possible advice (as in fact
he did), and you had lapsed into indolence and paid no attention to it, would the city have achieved any of the results
which followed on that occasion ? Impossible ! And so it
is with all that I say to-day, and with all that this or that
speaker may say. For the actions you must look to yourselves ;
from the speaker you must require that he give you the best
counsel that he can.[n]

76   I desire now to sum up my advice and to leave the platform.
I say that we must contribute funds, and must keep together
the force now in existence, correcting anything that may
seem amiss in it, but not disbanding the whole force because
of the possible criticisms against it. We must send envoys
everywhere to instruct, to warn, and to act. Above all,
we must punish those who take bribes in connexion with
public affairs, and must everywhere display our abhorrence
of them ; in order that reasonable men, who offer their

honest services, may find their policy justified in their own eyes and in those of others. If you treat the situation thus, 77 and cease to ignore it altogether, there is a chance—a chance I say, even now—that it may improve. If, however, you sit idle, with an interest that stops short at applause and acclamation, and retires into the background when any action is required, I can imagine no oratory, which, without action on your part, will be able to save your country.

THE THIRD PHILIPPIC (Or. IX)

[*Introduction.* The Third Philippic seems to have been delivered in the late spring or early summer of 341 B.C., about two months after the Speech on the Chersonese, which apparently had little positive result, though it probably prevented the recall and prosecution of Diopeithes. The immediate occasion of the Third Philippic was a request from the forces in the Chersonese for supplies. The general situation is the same as at the date of the last speech, but the danger to Byzantium is more pressing. Demosthenes now takes the broad ground of Panhellenic policy, and formally proposes to send envoys throughout Greece, to unite all the Greek states against Philip, as well as to send immediate reinforcements and supplies to the Chersonese.

Many critics, ancient and modern, have regarded this as the greatest of all Demosthenes' political orations. The lessons of history (from the speaker's point of view) are repeated and enforced by the citation of instance after instance. The tone of the speech, while less varied than that of the last, is grave and intense. The passage (§§ 36 ff.) in which the orator contrasts the spirit of Athenian political life in the past with that of his own day is one of the most impressive in all his works, and the nobility of his appeal to the traditional ideals of Athenian policy has been universally recognized even by his most severe critics.

The speech is found in the MSS. in two forms, of which the shorter omits a number of passages [1] which the longer includes, though there are signs of an imperfect blending of the two versions in certain places. It seems probable that both versions are due to Demosthenes, and the speech

---

[1] These are printed in square brackets in the translation.

may have been more than once revised by him before publica-
tion or republication. In which form it was delivered there
is not sufficient evidence to show.]

MANY speeches are made, men of Athens, at almost every 1
meeting of the Assembly, with reference to the aggressions
which Philip has been committing, ever since he concluded
the Peace, not only against yourselves but against all other
peoples ; and I am sure that all would agree, however little
they may act on their belief, that our aim, both in speech
and in action, should be to cause him to cease from his
insolence and to pay the penalty for it. And yet I see that
in fact the treacherous sacrifice of our interests has gone
on, until what seems an ill-omened saying may, I fear, be
really true—that if all who came forward desired to propose,
and you desired to carry, the measures which would make
your position as pitiful as it could possibly be, it could not
(so I believe), be made worse than it is now. It may be that 2
there are many reasons for this, and that our affairs did not
reach their present condition from any one or two causes.
But if you examine the matter aright, you will find that the
chief responsibility rests with those whose aim is to win your
favour, not to propose what is best. Some of them, men of
Athens, so long as they can maintain the conditions which
bring them reputation and influence, take no thought for the
future [and therefore think that you also should take none];
while others, by accusing and slandering those who are
actively at work,[n] are simply trying to make the city spend its
energies in punishing the members of its own body, and so
leave Philip free to say and do what he likes. Such political 3
methods as these, familiar to you as they are, are the real causes
of the evil. And I beg you, men of Athens, if I tell you certain

truths outspokenly, to let no resentment on your part fall
upon me on this account. Consider the matter in this light.
In every other sphere of life, you believe that the right of
free speech ought to be so universally shared by all who are
in the city, that you have extended it both to foreigners
and to slaves ; and one may see many a servant in Athens
speaking his mind with greater liberty than is granted to
citizens in some other states : but from the sphere of political
4 counsel you have utterly banished this liberty. The result [n]
is that in your meetings you give yourselves airs and enjoy
their flattery, listening to nothing but what is meant to
please you, while in the world of facts and events, you
are in the last extremity of peril. If then you are still
in this mood to-day, I do not know what I can say ;
but if you are willing to listen while I tell you, without
flattery, what your interest requires, I am prepared to speak.
For though our position is very bad indeed, and much has been
sacrificed, it is still possible, even now, if you will do your
5 duty, to set all right once more. It is a strange thing, perhaps,
that I am about to say, but it is true. The worst feature in
the past is that in which lies our best hope for the future.
And what is this ? It is that you are in your present plight
because you do not do any part of your duty, small or great ;
for of course, if you were doing all that you should do, and
were still in this evil case, you could not even hope for any
improvement. As it is, Philip has conquered your indolence
and your indifference ; but he has not conquered Athens.
You have not been vanquished—you have never even stirred.
6   [Now if it was admitted by us all that Philip was at war
with Athens, and was transgressing the Peace, a speaker would
have to do nothing but to advise you as to the safest and

easiest method of resistance to him. But since there are some
who are in so extraordinary a frame of mind that, though
he is capturing cities, though many of your possessions are
in his hands, and though he is committing aggressions against
all men, they still tolerate certain speakers, who constantly
assert at your meetings that it is some of *us* who are provoking
the war, it is necessary to be on our guard and come to a right
understanding on the matter. For there is a danger lest **7**
any one who proposes or advises resistance should find himself
accused of having brought about the war.]

[Well, I say this first of all, and lay it down as a principle,
that if it is open to us to deliberate whether we should remain
at peace or should go to war . . .]

Now if it is possible for the city to remain at peace—if the **8**
decision rests with us (that I may make this my starting-point)
—then, I say that we ought to do so, and I call upon any one
who says that it is so to move his motion, and to act and not
to defraud us.[n] But if another with weapons in his hands
and a large force about him holds out to you the *name* of
peace, while his own acts are acts of war, what course remains
open to us but that of resistance? though if you wish to
profess peace in the same manner as he, I have no quarrel
with you. But if any man's conception of peace is that it **9**
is a state in which Philip can master all that intervenes till
at last he comes to attack ourselves, such a conception, in
the first place, is madness; and, in the second place, this
peace that he speaks of is a peace which you are to observe
towards Philip, while he does not observe it towards you :
and this it is—this power to carry on war against you,
without being met by any hostilities on your part—that
Philip is purchasing with all the money that he is spending.

10 Indeed, if we intend to wait till the time comes when he admits that he is at war with us, we are surely the most innocent persons in the world. Why, even if he comes to Attica itself, to the very Peiraeus, he will never make such an admission, if we are to judge by his dealings with others.

11 For, to take one instance, he told the Olynthians, when he was five miles from the city, that there were only two alternatives—either they must cease to live in Olynthus, or he to live in Macedonia: but during the whole time before that, whenever any one accused him of any such sentiments, he was indignant and sent envoys to answer the charge. Again, he marched into the Phocians' country, as though visiting his allies : [n] it was by Phocian envoys that he was escorted on the march ; and most people in Athens contended strongly that his crossing the Pass would bring no good to

12 Thebes.   Worse still, he has lately seized Pherae [n] and still holds it, though he went to Thessaly as a friend and an ally. And, latest of all, he told those unhappy citizens of Oreus [n] that he had sent his soldiers to visit them and to make kind inquiries ; he had heard that they were sick, and suffering from faction, and it was right for an ally and a true friend

13 to be present at such a time.   Now if, instead of giving them warning and using open force, he deliberately chose to deceive these men, who could have done him no harm, though they might have taken precautions against suffering any themselves, do you imagine that he will make a formal declaration of war upon you before he commences hostilities,

14 and that, so long as you are content to be deceived ?   Impossible !   For so long as you, though you are the injured party, make no complaint against him, but accuse some of your own body, he would be the most fatuous man

on earth if *he* were to interrupt your strife and contentions
with one another—to bid you turn upon himself, and so to
cut away the ground from the arguments by which his
hirelings put you off, when they tell you that *he* is not at
war with Athens.

In God's name, is there a man in his senses who would 15
judge by words, and not by facts, whether another was at
peace or at war with him ? Of course there is not. Why,
from the very first, when the Peace had only just been made,
before those who are now in the Chersonese had been sent out,
Philip was taking Serrhium [n] and Doriscus, and expelling
the soldiers who were in the castle of Serrhium and the Sacred
Mountain, where they had been placed by your general.
But what was he doing, in acting thus ? For he had sworn 16
to a Peace.[n] And let no one ask, ' What do these things
amount to ? What do they matter to Athens ? ' For whether
these acts were trifles which could have no interest for you
is another matter ; but the principles of religion [n] and
justice, whether a man transgress them in small things or
great, have always the same force. What ? When he is
sending mercenaries into the Chersonese, which the king
and all the Hellenes have acknowledged to be yours ; when
he openly avows that he is going to the rescue, and states
it in his letter, what is it that he is doing ? He tells you, 17
indeed, that he is not making war upon you. But so far am I
from admitting that one who acts in this manner is observing
the Peace which he made with you, that I hold that in
grasping at Megara, in setting up tyrants in Euboea, in
advancing against Thrace at the present moment, in pursuing
his machinations in the Peloponnese, and in carrying out his
entire policy with the help of his army, he is violating the

Peace and is making war against you ;—unless you mean
to say that even to bring up engines to besiege you is no
breach of the Peace, until they are actually planted against
your walls. But you will not say this ; for the man who is
taking the steps and contriving the means which will lead
to my capture is at war with me, even though he has not
18 yet thrown a missile or shot an arrow. Now what are the
things which would imperil your safety, if anything should
happen ? [n] The alienation of the Hellespont, the placing of
Megara and Euboea in the power of the enemy, and the
attraction of Peloponnesian sympathy to his cause. Can
I then say that one who is erecting such engines of war as
19 these against the city is at peace with you ? Far from it !
For from the very day when he annihilated the Phocians—
from that very day, I say, I date the beginning of his hostilities
against you. And for your part, I think that you will be wise
if you resist him at once ; but that if you let him be, you will
find that, when you wish to resist, resistance itself is impossible.
Indeed, so widely do I differ, men of Athens, from all your
other advisers, that I do not think there is any room for
discussion to-day in regard to the Chersonese or Byzantium.
20 We *must* go to their defence, and take every care that they
do not suffer [and we must send all that they need to the
soldiers who are at present there]. But we *have* to take
counsel for the good of all the Hellenes, in view of the grave
peril in which they stand. And I wish to tell you on what
grounds I am so alarmed at the situation, in order that if my
reasoning is correct, you may share my conclusions, and
exercise some forethought for yourselves at least, if you are
actually unwilling to do so for the Hellenes as a whole ;
but that if you think that I am talking nonsense, and am

out of my senses, you may both now and hereafter decline
to attend to me as though I were a sane man.

The rise of Philip to greatness from such small and humble 21
beginnings ; the mistrustful and quarrelsome attitude of the
Hellenes towards one another ; the fact that his growth out
of what he was into what he is was a far more extraordinary
thing than would be his subjugation of all that remains,
when he has already secured so much ;—all this and all
similar themes, upon which I might speak at length, I will
pass over. But I see that all men, beginning with yourselves, 22
have conceded to him the very thing which has been at issue
in every Hellenic war during the whole of the past. And
what is this ? It is the right to act as he pleases—to mutilate
and to strip the Hellenic peoples, one by one, to attack
and to enslave their cities. For seventy-three years [n] you 23
were the leading people of Hellas, and the Spartans for thirty
years save one ; [n] and in these last times, after the battle
of Leuctra,[n] the Thebans too acquired some power : yet
neither to you nor to Thebes nor to Sparta was such a right
ever conceded by the Hellenes, as the right to do whatever
you pleased. Far from it ! First of all it was your own 24
behaviour—or rather that of the Athenians of that day—
which some thought immoderate ; and all, even those who
had no grievance against Athens, felt bound to join the
injured parties, and to make war upon you. Then, in their
turn, the Spartans, when they had acquired an empire and
succeeded to a supremacy like your own, attempted to go
beyond all bounds and to disturb the established order [n]
to an unjustifiable extent ; and once more, all, even those
who had no grievance against them, had recourse to war.
Why mention the others ? For we ourselves and the Spartans, 25

though we could originally allege no injury done by the one
people to the other, nevertheless felt bound to go to war
on account of the wrongs which we saw the rest suffering.
And yet all the offences of the Spartans in those thirty years
of power, and of your ancestors in their seventy years, were
less, men of Athens, than the wrongs inflicted upon the Greeks
by Philip, in the thirteen years, not yet completed, during
26 which he has been to the fore. Less do I say ? They are
not a fraction of them. [A few words will easily prove this.]
I say nothing of Olynthus, and Methone, and Apollonia, and
thirty-two cities in the Thracian region,[n] all annihilated by
him with such savagery, that a visitor to the spot would
find it difficult to tell that they had ever been inhabited.
I remain silent in regard to the extirpation of the great
Phocian race. But what is the condition of Thessaly ? Has
he not robbed their very cities of their governments,[n] and
set up tetrarchies, that they may be enslaved, not merely
27 by whole cities, but by whole tribes at a time ? Are not the
cities of Euboea even now ruled by tyrants, and that in an
island that is neighbour to Thebes and Athens ? Does he
not write expressly in his letters, ' I am at peace with those
who choose to obey me ' ? And what he thus writes he does
not fail to act upon ; for he is gone to invade the Hellespont ;
he previously went to attack Ambracia ; [n] the great city of
Elis [n] in the Peloponnese is his ; he has recently intrigued
against Megara ; [n] and neither Hellas nor the world beyond
28 it is large enough to contain the man's ambition. But though
all of us, the Hellenes, see and hear these things, we send no
representatives to one another to discuss the matter ; we
show no indignation ; we are in so evil a mood, so deep
have the lines been dug which sever city from city, that up

to this very day we are unable to act as either our interest or our duty require. We cannot unite; we can form no 29 combination for mutual support or friendship; but we look on while the man grows greater, because every one has made up his mind (as it seems to me) to profit by the time during which his neighbour is being ruined, and no one cares or acts for the safety of the Hellenes. For we all know that Philip is like the recurrence or the attack of a fever or other illness, in his descent upon those who fancy themselves for the present well out of his reach. And further, you must 30 surely realize that all the wrongs that the Hellenes suffered from the Spartans or ourselves they at least suffered at the hands of true-born sons of Hellas; and (one might conceive) it was as though a lawful son, born to a great estate, managed his affairs in some wrong or improper way;—his conduct would in itself deserve blame and denunciation, but at least it could not be said that he was not one of the family, or was not the heir to the property. But had it been a slave 31 or a supposititious son that was thus ruining and spoiling an inheritance to which he had no title, why, good Heavens! how infinitely more scandalous and reprehensible all would have declared it to be. And yet they show no such feeling in regard to Philip, although not only is he no Hellene, not only has he no kinship with Hellenes, but he is not even a barbarian from a country that one could acknowledge with credit;—he is a pestilent Macedonian, from whose country it used not to be possible to buy even a slave of any value.

And in spite of this, is there any degree of insolence to 32 which he does not proceed? Not content with annihilating cities, does he not manage the Pythian games,[n] the common meeting of the Hellenes, and send his slaves to preside over the competition in his absence ? [Is he not master of Thermopylae, and of the passes which lead into Hellenic territory ? Does he not hold that district with garrisons and mercenaries ? Has he not taken the precedence in consulting the oracle, and thrust aside ourselves and the Thessalians and Dorians and the rest of the Amphictyons, though the right is not one which

33 is given even to all of the Hellenes ?] Does he not write to the Thessalians to prescribe the constitution under which they are to live ? Does he not send one body of mercenaries to Porthmus, to expel the popular party of Eretria, and another to Oreus, to set up Philistides as tyrant ? And yet the Hellenes see these things and endure them, gazing (it seems to me) as they would gaze at a hailstorm—each people praying that it may not come their way, but no one trying to prevent it. Nor is it only his outrages upon Hellas that go unresisted.

34 No one resists even the aggressions which are committed against himself. Ambracia and Leucas belong to the Corinthians—he has attacked them : Naupactus to the Achaeans—he has sworn to hand it over to the Aetolians : Echinus [n] to the Thebans—he has taken it from them, and is now march-

35 ing against their allies the Byzantines—is it not so ? And of our own possessions, to pass by all the rest, is not Cardia, the greatest city in the Chersonese, in his hands ? Thus are we treated ; and we are all hesitating and torpid, with our eyes upon our neighbours, distrusting one another, rather than the man whose victims we all are. But if he treats us collectively in this outrageous fashion, what do you think he will do, when he has become master of each of us separately ?

36   What then is the cause of these things ? For as it was not without reason and just cause that the Hellenes in old days

were so prompt for freedom, so it is not without reason
or cause that they are now so prompt to be slaves. There
was a spirit, men of Athens, a spirit in the minds of the people
in those days, which is absent to-day—the spirit which vanquished the wealth of Persia, which led Hellas in the path
of freedom, and never gave way in face of battle by sea or by
land ; a spirit whose extinction to-day has brought universal
ruin and turned Hellas upside down. What was this spirit ?
[It was nothing subtle nor clever.] It meant that men who **37**
took money from those who aimed at dominion or at the ruin
of Hellas were execrated by all ; that it was then a very
grave thing to be convicted of bribery ; that the punishment
for the guilty man was the heaviest that could be inflicted ;
that for him there could be no plea for mercy, nor hope of
pardon. No orator, no general, would then sell the critical **38**
opportunity whenever it arose—the opportunity so often
offered to men by fortune, even when they are careless and
their foes are on their guard. They did not barter away
the harmony between people and people, nor their own
mistrust of the tyrant and the foreigner, nor any of these
high sentiments. Where are such sentiments now ? They **39**
have been sold in the market and are gone; and those have
been imported in their stead, through which the nation lies
ruined and plague-stricken—the envy of the man who has
received his hire ; the amusement which accompanies his
avowal ; [the pardon granted to those whose guilt is proved;]
the hatred of one who censures the crime ; and all the
appurtenances of corruption. For as to ships, numerical **40**
strength, unstinting abundance of funds and all other material
of war, and all the things by which the strength of cities is
estimated, every people can command these in greater
plenty and on a larger scale by far than in old days. But

all these resources are rendered unserviceable, ineffectual, unprofitable, by those who traffic in them.

41   That these things are so to-day, you doubtless see, and need no testimony of mine : and that in times gone by the opposite was true, I will prove to you, not by any words of my own, but by the record inscribed by your ancestors on a pillar of bronze, and placed on the Acropolis [not to be a lesson to themselves—they needed no such record to put them in a right mind—but to be a reminder and an example to you

42 of the zeal that you ought to display in such a cause]. What then is the record ? ' Arthmius,[n] son of Pythonax, of Zeleia, is an outlaw, and is the enemy of the Athenian people and their allies, he and his house.' Then follows the reason for which this step was taken—' because he brought the gold

43 from the Medes into the Peloponnese.' Such is the record. Consider, in Heaven's name, what must have been the mind of the Athenians of that day, when they did this, and their conception of their position. They set up a record, that because a man of Zeleia, Arthmius by name, a slave of the King of Persia (for Zeleia is in Asia), as part of his service to the king, had brought gold, not to Athens, but to the Peloponnese, he should be an enemy of Athens and her allies, he and his house, and that they should be outlaws. And

44 this outlawry is no such disfranchisement as we ordinarily mean by the word. For what would it matter to a man of Zeleia, that he might have no share in the public life of Athens ? But there is a clause in the Law of Murder, dealing with those in connexion with whose death the law does not allow a prosecution for murder [but the slaying of them is to be a holy act]: ' And let him die an outlaw,' it runs. The meaning, accordingly, is this—that the slayer of such

a man is to be pure from all guilt. They thought, therefore, 45
that the safety of all the Hellenes was a matter which concerned themselves—apart from this belief, it could not have
mattered to them whether any one bought or corrupted
men in the Peloponnese ; and whenever they detected
such offenders, they carried their punishment and their
vengeance so far as to pillory their names for ever. As
the natural consequence, the Hellenes were a terror to the
foreigner, not the foreigner to the Hellenes. It is not so
now. Such is not your attitude in these or in other matters.
But what is it ? [You know it yourselves ; for why should 46
I accuse you explicitly on every point ? And that of the rest
of the Hellenes is like your own, and no better ; and so I say
that the present situation demands our utmost earnestness
and good counsel.[n]] And what counsel ? Do you bid me
tell you, and will you not be angry if I do so ?

[*He reads from the document.*]

Now there is an ingenuous argument, which is used by 47
those who would reassure the city, to the effect that, after
all, Philip is not yet in the position once held by the Spartans,
who ruled everywhere over sea and land, with the king for
their ally, and nothing to withstand them ; and that, none
the less, Athens defended herself even against them, and was
not swept away. Since that time the progress in every
direction, one may say, has been great, and has made the
world to-day very different from what it was then ; but I
believe that in no respect has there been greater progress
or development than in the art of war. In the first place, 48
I am told that in those days the Spartans and all our other
enemies would invade us for four or five months—during,

that is, the actual summer—and would damage Attica with infantry and citizen-troops, and then return home again. And so old-fashioned were the men of that day—nay rather, such true citizens—that no one ever purchased any object from another for money, but their warfare was of a legitimate

49 and open kind. But now, as I am sure you see, most of our losses are the result of treachery, and no issue is decided by open conflict or battle; while you are told that it is not because he leads a column of heavy infantry [n] that Philip can march wherever he chooses, but because he has attached to himself a force of light infantry, cavalry, archers, mercenaries,

50 and similar troops. And whenever, with such advantages,[n] he falls upon a State which is disordered within, and in their distrust of one another no one goes out in defence of its territory, he brings up his engines and besieges them. I pass over the fact that summer and winter are alike to him— that there is no close season during which he suspends

51 operations. But if you all know these things and take due account of them, you surely must not let the war pass into Attica, nor be dashed from your seat through looking back to the simplicity of those old hostilities with Sparta. You must guard against him, at the greatest possible distance, both by political measures and by preparations; you must prevent his stirring from home, instead of grappling with him

52 at close quarters in a struggle to the death. For, men of Athens, we have many natural advantages for a war,[n] if we are willing to do our duty. There is the character of his country, much of which we can harry and damage, and a thousand other things. But for a pitched battle he is in better training than we.

53   Nor have you only to recognize these facts, and to resist

him by actual operations of war. You must also by reasoned
judgement and of set purpose come to execrate those who
address you in his interest, remembering that it is impossible
to master the enemies of the city, until you punish those
who are serving them in the city itself. And this, before 54
God and every Heavenly Power—this you will not be able
to do ; for you have reached such a pitch of folly or dis-
traction or—I know not what to call it ; for often has the
fear actually entered my mind, that some more than mortal
power may be driving our fortunes to ruin—that to enjoy
their abuse, or their malice, or their jests, or whatever your
motive may chance to be, you call upon men to speak who
are hirelings, and some of whom would not even deny it ;
and you laugh to hear their abuse of others. And terrible as 55
this is, there is yet worse to be told. For you have actually
made political life safer for these men, than for those who
uphold your own cause. And yet observe what calamities
the willingness to listen to such men lays up in store. I will
mention facts known to you all.

In Olynthus, among those who were engaged in public 56
affairs, there was one party who were on the side of Philip,
and served his interests in everything ; and another whose
aim was their city's real good, and the preservation of their
fellow citizens from bondage. Which were the destroyers
of their country ? which betrayed the cavalry, through whose
betrayal Olynthus perished ? Those whose sympathies were
with Philip's cause ; those who, while the city still existed
brought such dishonest and slanderous charges against the
speakers whose advice was for the best, that, in the case of
Apollonides at least, the people of Olynthus was even induced
to banish the accused.

57 Nor is this instance of the unmixed evil wrought by these practices in the case of the Olynthians an exceptional one, or without parallel elsewhere. For in Eretria,[n] when Plutarchus and the mercenaries had been got rid of, and the people had control of the city and of Porthmus, one party wished to entrust the State to you, the other to entrust it to Philip. And through listening mainly, or rather entirely, to the latter, these poor luckless Eretrians were at last persuaded to banish the advocates of their own interests.

58 For, as you know, Philip, their ally, sent Hipponicus with a thousand mercenaries, stripped Porthmus of its walls, and set up three tyrants—Hipparchus, Automedon, and Cleitarchus; and since then he has already twice expelled them from the country when they wished to recover their position [sending on the first occasion the mercenaries commanded by Eurylochus, on the second, those under Parmenio].

59 And why go through the mass of the instances ? Enough to mention how in Oreus Philip had, as his agents, Philistides, Menippus, Socrates, Thoas, and Agapaeus—the very men who are now in possession of the city—and every one knew the fact ; while a certain Euphraeus,[n] who once lived here in Athens, acted in the interests of freedom, to save his

60 country from bondage. To describe the insults and the contumely with which he met would require a long story ; but a year before the capture of the town he laid an information of treason against Philistides and his party, having perceived the nature of their plans. A number of men joined forces, with Philip for their paymaster and director, and haled Euphraeus off to prison as a disturber of the peace.

61 Seeing this, the democratic party in Oreus, instead of coming to the rescue of Euphraeus, and beating the other

party to death, displayed no anger at all against them, and agreed with a malicious pleasure that Euphraeus deserved his fate. After this the conspirators worked with all the freedom they desired for the capture of the city, and made arrangements for the execution of the scheme; while any of the democratic party, who perceived what was going on, maintained a panic-stricken silence, remembering the fate of Euphraeus. So wretched was their condition, that though this dreadful calamity was confronting them, no one dared open his lips, until all was ready and the enemy was advancing up to the walls. Then the one party set about the defence, the other about the betrayal of the city. And when the city 62 had been captured in this base and shameful manner, the successful party governed despotically: and of those who had been their own protectors, and had been ready to treat Euphraeus with all possible harshness, they expelled some and murdered others; while the good Euphraeus killed himself, thus testifying to the righteousness and purity of his motives in opposing Philip on behalf of his countrymen.

Now for what reason, you may be wondering, were the 63 peoples of Olynthus and Eretria and Oreus more agreeably disposed towards Philip's advocates than towards their own? The reason was the same as it is with you—that those who speak for your true good can never, even if they would, speak to win popularity with you; they are constrained to inquire how the State may be saved: while their opponents, in the very act of seeking popularity, are co-operating with Philip. The one party said, 'You must pay taxes;' the 64 other, 'There is no need to do so.' The one said, 'Go to war, and do not trust him;' the other, ' Remain at peace,'—until they were in the toils. And—not to mention each separately

—I believe that the same thing was true of all. The one side said what would enable them to win favour ; the other, what would secure the safety of their State. And at last the main body of the people accepted much that they proposed—not now from any such desire for gratification, nor from ignorance, but as a concession to circumstances, 65 thinking that their cause was now wholly lost. It is this fate, I solemnly assure you, that I dread for you, when the time comes that you make your reckoning, and realize that there is no longer anything that can be done. May you never find yourselves, men of Athens, in such a position ! Yet in any case, it were better to die ten thousand deaths, than to do anything out of servility towards Philip [or to sacrifice any of those who speak for your good]. A noble recompense did the people in Oreus receive, for entrusting themselves to Philip's friends, and thrusting Euphraeus 66 aside ! and a noble recompense the democracy of Eretria, for driving away your envoys, and surrendering to Cleitarchus ! They are slaves, scourged and butchered ! A noble clemency did he show to the Olynthians, who elected Lasthenes to command the cavalry, and banished Apollonides ! 67 It is folly, and it is cowardice, to cherish hopes like these, to give way to evil counsels, to refuse to do anything that you should do, to listen to the advocates of the enemy's cause, and to fancy that you dwell in so great a city that, whatever 68 happens, you will not suffer any harm. Aye, and it is shameful to exclaim after the event, ' Why, who would have expected this ? Of course, we ought to have done, or not to have done, such and such things ! ' The Olynthians could tell you of many things, to have foreseen which in time would have saved them from destruction. So too could the people

of Oreus, and the Phocians, and every other people that has
been destroyed. But how does that help them now? So 69
long as the vessel is safe, be it great or small, so long must
the sailor and the pilot and every man in his place exert himself and take care that no one may capsize it by design or by
accident : but when the seas have overwhelmed it, all their
efforts are in vain. So it is, men of Athens, with us. While 70
we are still safe, with our great city, our vast resources, our
noble name, what are we to do? Perhaps some one sitting
here has long been wishing to ask this question. Aye, and
I will answer it, and will move my motion ; and you shall
carry it, if you wish. We ourselves, in the first place, must
conduct the resistance and make preparation for it—with
ships, that is, and money, and soldiers. For though all but
ourselves give way and become slaves, we at least must
contend for freedom. And when we have made all these 71
preparations ourselves, and let them be seen, then let us
call upon the other states for aid, and send envoys to carry
our message [in all directions—to the Peloponnese, to Rhodes,
to Chios, to the king ; for it is not unimportant for his
interests either that Philip should be prevented from sub-
jugating the world] ; that so, if you persuade them, you may
have partners to share the danger and the expense, in case
of need ; and if you do not, you may at least delay the
march of events. For since the war is with a single 72
man, and not against the strength of a united state, even
delay is not without its value, any more than were those
embassies [n] of protest which last year went round the
Peloponnese, when I and Polyeuctus, that best of men, and
Hegesippus and the other envoys went on our tour, and
forced him to halt, so that he neither went to attack

73 Acarnania, nor set out for the Peloponnese. But I do not
mean that we should call upon the other states, if we are
not willing to take any of the necessary steps ourselves. It is
folly to sacrifice what is our own, and then pretend to be
anxious for the interests of others—to neglect the present,
and alarm others in regard to the future. I do not propose
this. I say that we must send money to the forces in the
Chersonese, and do all that they ask of us ; that we must
make preparation ourselves, while we summon, convene,
instruct, and warn the rest of the Hellenes. That is the
74 policy for a city with a reputation such as yours. But if you
fancy that the people of Chalcis or of Megara will save Hellas,
while you run away from the task, you are mistaken. They
may well be content if they can each save themselves. The
task is yours. It is the prerogative that your forefathers
won, and through many a great peril bequeathed to you.

75 But if each of you is to sit and consult his inclinations, looking
for some way by which he may escape any personal action,
the first consequence will be that you will never find any one
who will act; and the second, I fear, that the day will come
when we shall be forced to do, at one and the same time,
all the things we wish to avoid.

76   This then is my proposal, and this I move. If the proposal
is carried out, I think that even now the state of our affairs
may be remedied. But if any one has a better proposal
to make, let him make it, and give us his advice. And I pray
to all the gods that whatever be the decision that you are
about to make, it may be for your good.

ON THE CROWN (Or. XVIII)

[*Introduction.* The advice given by Demosthenes in the Third Philippic (spoken before the middle of 341) was in the main followed. He himself was sent almost immediately to Byzantium, where he renewed the alliance between that city and Athens, and at the same time entered into relations with Abydos and the Thracian princes. Rhodes, and probably Chios and Cos, were also conciliated, and an embassy was sent to the King of Persia to ask for aid against Philip. The king appears to have sent assistance to Diopeithes, and it is also stated (not on the best authority) that he sent large sums of money to Demosthenes and Hypereides. Demosthenes further succeeded, in conjunction with Callias of Chalcis, in organizing a league against Philip, which included Corinth, Megara, Corcyra, and the Acarnanians, and which at least supplied a considerable number of men and some funds. The cities of Euboea, most of which had been in the hands of Philip's party, were also formed into a confederacy, in alliance with Athens, under the leadership of Chalcis; Philistides was expelled from Oreus, about July 341, by the allied forces under Cephisophon; and later in the summer, Phocion drove Cleitarchus from Eretria. On the motion of Aristonicus, the Athenians voted Demosthenes a golden crown, which was conferred on him in the theatre at the Great Dionysia in March 340. The arrest of Anaxinus of Oreus, and his condemnation as a spy, acting in Philip's interest, must have occurred about the same time. Not long afterwards Demosthenes succeeded in carrying out a complete reorganization of the trierarchic system, by which he made the burden of the expense vary strictly according to property, and secured a regular and efficient supply of ships, money, and men.

In the meantime (in 341 or 340) the island of Peparethus

was attacked by Philip's ships, in revenge for the seizure of
the Macedonian garrison in Halonnesus by the Peparethians :
and the Athenian admirals were ordered to retaliate. Philip
himself had been pursuing his course in Thrace ; and on the
rejection of his request to Byzantium for an alliance, he laid
siege (late in 340) to Perinthus (which lay on his way to Byzantium), sending part of his forces through the Chersonese.
Aided by Byzantine and Persian soldiers, Perinthus held out,
till at last Philip took off most of his forces and besieged
Byzantium itself. He had shortly before this sent to Athens
an express declaration of war, and received a similar declaration from her, the formal excuse for which was found in
the recent seizure by his ships of some Athenian merchant-
vessels. But with help from Athens, Chios, Rhodes, and
Cos, the Byzantines maintained the defence. Philip's position became serious ; but he managed by a ruse to get his
ships away into the open sea, and even to do some damage
to the Athenian settlers in the Chersonese. In the winter
he withdrew from Byzantium, and in 339 made an incursion
into Scythia ; but, returning through the country of the
Triballi, he sustained some loss, and was severely wounded.
Later in the year a new Sacred War which had arisen gave
him a convenient opportunity for the invasion of Greece.

At the meeting of the Amphictyonic Council in the autumn
of 340,[1] Aeschines was one of the representatives of Athens.
The Athenians had recently offended Thebes by re-gilding
and dedicating in the restored temple at Delphi fifty shields,
with an inscription stating that they were spoil ' taken from
the Medes and the Thebans, when they fought against the
Hellenes ' (probably at Plataeae in 479). The Locrians of
Amphissa intended (according to Aeschines' account) to
propose that the Council should fine Athens fifty talents.
Aeschines rose to state the case for Athens ; but a delegate
from Amphissa forbade all mention of the Athenians, and

[1] Some writers suppose that it was at the meeting in the spring of
339. The evidence is not conclusive, but appears to point to the date
given here.

demanded their exclusion from the temple, on the ground
of their alliance with the accursed Phocians. Aeschines
retorted by charging the Amphisseans with cultivating and
building upon the sacred plain of Cirrha—acts forbidden
for all time in 586 B.C.—and roused the Council to such
indignation that they gathered a body of men and destroyed
the harbour and the unlawful buildings of Cirrha ; but they
were severely handled by the Amphisseans, and the Council
now voted that the Amphictyonic states should send representatives, to discuss the question of war against Amphissa,
to a meeting to be held at Thermopylae before the spring
meeting of the Council. To this preliminary meeting, the
Athenians (though inclined to view Aeschines' performance
with favour), on the advice of Demosthenes, sent no representatives ; nor did the Thebans (the allies of Amphissa).
War was declared by the Amphictyons against Amphissa ;
but Cottyphus, the Thessalian, who had been appointed
general, made little headway, and (at the spring or the
autumn meeting of the Council) declared that the Amphictyonic states must either send men and money, or
else make Philip their general. Philip was, of course,
at once appointed ; but instead of proceeding against Amphissa, marched to Elateia and fortified it. This caused
the greatest alarm at Athens. Demosthenes was immediately
dispatched to Thebes, where he succeeded, by what appear
to have been liberal and judicious proposals, in making an
alliance between Thebes and Athens, in spite of the attempts
of Philip's envoys to counteract his influence. Euboea,
Megara, Corinth, and other members of the league also
sent help. Philip himself called upon his own friends in
the Peloponnese for aid, and at last moved towards Amphissa. Demosthenes seems now to have succeeded in apply-
ing the festival-money to purposes of war, and with the aid of
Lycurgus, who became Controller of the Festival Fund, to have
amassed a large sum for the use of the State. At the Dionysia
of 338 he was again crowned, on the proposal of Demomeles
and Hypereides. The allies at first won some successes and

refortified some of the Phocian towns, but afterwards unfortunately divided their forces, and so enabled Philip to defeat the two divisions separately, and to destroy Amphissa. Philip's proposals of peace found supporters both in Thebes and in Athens, but were counteracted by Demosthenes. Late in the summer of 338, the decisive battle was fought at Chaeroneia, and resulted in the total rout of the allies. Demosthenes himself was one of the fugitives. Philip placed a Macedonian garrison in Thebes, restored his exiled friends to power there, established a Council of Three Hundred, and (through them) put to death or banished his enemies. He also gave Orchomenus, Thespiae, and Plataeae their independence. After a moment of panic, the Athenians, led by Demosthenes, Lycurgus, and Hypereides, proceeded to take all possible measures for the defence of the city, while private munificence supplied the treasury. Demosthenes himself superintended the repair of the fortifications, and went on a mission to secure a supply of corn. But Philip, instead of marching upon Athens, sent a message by Demades, whom he had taken prisoner at Chaeroneia; and the Assembly, in reply, instructed Demades, Aeschines, and Phocion to ask Philip to release his Athenian prisoners. Philip released them without ransom, and sent Antipater and Alexander (with the ashes of the Athenian dead) to offer terms of peace. By the ' Peace of Demades ', concluded while Demosthenes was still absent, the alliance between Athens and Philip was renewed; the independence of Athens was guaranteed; Oropus was taken from Thebes and restored to Athens; and she was permitted to retain Salamis, Samos, Delos, and probably Lemnos and Imbros. On the other hand, she lost all her possessions on the Hellespont and in the Chersonese, and promised to join the league which Philip intended to form for the invasion of Persia. Demosthenes was selected by the Assembly to deliver the funeral oration upon those who fell at Chaeroneia; and although the Macedonian party attacked him repeatedly in the law-courts, he was always acquitted. Philip paid a long visit to the Peloponnese, in the course of which he placed a Macedonian garrison in Corinth, ravaged Laconia, giving parts of it to his allies, the Argives and Arcadians, and announced his plans for the invasion of Persia at the head of the Greeks : he then returned to Macedonia.

In 337 Demosthenes was again Commissioner of Fortifications, as well as Controller of the Festival Fund—the most important office in the State. He not only performed his work most efficiently, but gave considerable sums for public purposes out of his private fortune ; and early in 336 Ctesiphon proposed, and the Council resolved, that he should once more be crowned at the Dionysia. But before the proposal could be brought before the Assembly, Aeschines indicted Ctesiphon for its alleged illegality. The trial did not take place until late in the summer of 330. We do not know the reason for so long a delay, but probably the events of the intervening time were such as to render the state of public feeling unfavourable to Aeschines. In 336 Philip was assassinated, and was succeeded by Alexander. In 335 Alexander destroyed Thebes, which had revolted, and sold its inhabitants into slavery. He also demanded from Athens the surrender of Demosthenes and other anti-Macedonian politicians and generals, but was persuaded to be content with the banishment of Charidemus and Ephialtes, and the promise of the prosecution of Demosthenes for using subsidies from Persia to help Thebes—a prosecution which was allowed to drop. From 334 onwards Alexander was pursuing his conquests in the East, and we know practically nothing of the history of Athens until the trial of Ctesiphon came on in 330.

Aeschines alleged against Ctesiphon (1) that it was illegal to propose to crown any one who had not passed his examination before the Board of Auditors at the end of his term of office ; and that Demosthenes, who had been Commissioner of Fortifications and Controller of the Festival Fund, was still in this position : (2) that it was illegal to proclaim the grant of a crown at the Dionysia, except in the case of crowns conferred by foreign states : (3) that it was illegal to insert untrue statements in the public records, and that the language in which Ctesiphon's decree described the political career of Demosthenes was untrue. On the first point Aeschines was almost certainly right : Demosthenes' defence is sophistical, and all that could really be said was that the rule had often been broken before. On the second point, certainty is impossible : the most probable view (though it also has its difficulties) is that there were two inconsistent laws, and that one of them permitted the proclamation in the theatre, if expressly voted by the people ; but the alleged illegality had certainly been often committed. The third point, which raised the question of the value to Athens of Demosthenes' whole political life, was that upon which the case really turned; and it is to this that Demosthenes devotes the greater part of his speech, breaking up his reply into convenient stages by discussions (of a far less happy description) of the other counts of the indictment, and of the character and career of Aeschines. As in the Speech on the Embassy, certain facts are misrepresented, and there are passages which are in bad taste ; but Demosthenes proves beyond doubt his unswerving loyalty to the high ideal of policy which he had formed for his country, and it is with good reason that parts of this speech have always been felt to reach a height of eloquence which has never been surpassed.

The jury acquitted Ctesiphon : and Aeschines, failing to obtain a fifth part of the votes, and thus incurring a heavy fine and the loss of some of the rights of a citizen, left Athens, and lived most of the remainder of his life at Rhodes.

The following is an analysis of the speech in outline :—

I. Introduction (§§ 1–8).
II. Defence against charges irrelevant to the indictment (§§ 9–52).
    (1) Introduction (§ 9).
    (2) Postponement of reply to charges against his private life (§§ 10, 11).
    (3) Reply to charges against his public life (§§ 12–52).

1 I PRAY first, men of Athens, to every god and goddess, that
the goodwill, which I ever feel towards this city and towards
all of you, may in equal measure be vouchsafed to me by you
at this present trial : and secondly—a prayer which especially
touches yourselves, your consciences, and your reputation—
that the gods may put it into your minds not to take counsel
of my adversary [n] in regard to the spirit in which you ought
2 to hear me (for that would surely be a cruel thing), but of the
laws and of your oath ; wherein besides all other precepts of
justice, this also is written—that you shall listen to both sides
with a like mind. And this means, not only that you should
have formed no prejudice, and should accord equal goodwill
to each, but also that you should give leave to every man who
pleads before you to adopt that order, and make that defence,
upon which he has resolved and fixed his choice.

3 I am in many respects at a disadvantage in the present
controversy, as compared with Aeschines ; and particularly,
men of Athens, in two points of importance. The first is
that I am not contending for the same stake as he. It is

not the same thing for me to lose your goodwill now, as it is for him to fail to win his case ; since for me—but I would say nothing unpleasant [n] at the opening of my address— I say only that Aeschines can well afford to risk this attack upon me. The second disadvantage lies in the natural and universal tendency of mankind to hear invective and denunciation with pleasure, and to be offended with those who praise themselves. And of the two courses in question, that 4 which contributes to men's pleasure has been given to Aeschines, and that which annoys (I may say) every one is left for me. If, to avoid giving such annoyance, I say nothing of all that I myself have done, it will be thought that I am unable to clear myself of the charges against me, or to show the grounds upon which I claim to deserve distinction. If, on the other hand, I proceed to speak of my past acts and my political life, I shall often be compelled to speak of myself. I will endeavour, then, to do this as modestly as possible; and for all that the necessities of the case compel me to say, the blame must in fairness be borne by the prosecutor, who initiated a trial of such a kind as this.

I think, men of Athens, that you would all admit that this 5 present trial equally concerns myself and Ctesiphon, and demands no less earnest attention from me than from him. For while it is a painful and a grievous thing for a man to be robbed of anything, particularly if it is at the hands of an enemy that this befalls him, it is especially so, when he is robbed of your goodwill and kindness, just in proportion as to win these is the greatest possible gain. And because 6 such is the issue at stake in the present trial, I request and entreat you all alike to give me, while I make my defence upon the charges that have been brought against me, a fair hearing, as you are commanded to do by the laws—those laws to which their original maker, your well-wisher and the People's friend, Solon, thought fit to give the sanction not of enactment only, but also of an oath on the part of those who

7 act as judges : not because he distrusted you (so at least it seems to me), but because he saw that a defendant cannot escape from the imputations and the slanders which fall with special force from the prosecutor, because he is the first to speak, unless each of you who sit in judgement, keeping his conscience pure in the sight of God, will receive the pleadings of the later speaker also with the same favour, and will thus, because his attention has been given equally and impartially to both sides, form his decision upon the case in its entirety.

8 And now, when I am about, as it seems, to render an account of my whole private life and public career, I would once more invoke the aid of the gods ; and in the presence of you all I pray, first, that the goodwill which I ever feel towards this city and towards all of you, may in equal measure be vouchsafed to me by you at this trial ; and secondly, that whatsoever judgement upon this present suit will conduce to your public reputation, and the purity of each man's conscience, that judgement they may put it into all your minds to give.

9 Now if Aeschines had confined his charges to the subject of the indictment, I too, in making my defence, would have dealt at once with the actual resolution of the Council. But since he has devoted no less a portion of his speech to the relation of other matters, and for the most part has spoken against me falsely, I think it is necessary, and at the same time just, that I should deal briefly, men of Athens, with

these, in order that none of you may be led by irrelevant arguments to listen less favourably to my pleas in answer to the
indictment itself.

As for his slanderous vituperation of my private life, mark 10
how straightforward and how just is the reply that I make.
If you know me as the man that he charged me with being
(for my life has been spent nowhere but in your own midst),
do not even suffer me to speak—no, not though my whole
public career has been one of transcendent merit—but rise
and condemn me without delay. But if, in your judgement
and belief, I am a better man than Aeschines, and come of
better men; if I and mine are no worse than any other
respectable persons (to use no offensive expression); then
do not trust him even in regard to other points, for it is
plain that all that he said was equally fictitious; but once
more accord to me to-day the goodwill which throughout
the past you have so often displayed towards me in previous
trials. Knave as you are,[n] Aeschines, you were assuredly 11
more fool than knave, when you thought that I should
dismiss all that I had to say with regard to my past acts and
political life, and should turn to meet the abuse that fell
from you. I shall not do so; I am not so brain-sick; but
I will review the falsehoods and the calumnies which you
uttered against my political career; and then, if the court
desires it, I will afterwards refer to the ribald language that
has been so incontinently used.

The offences charged against me are many; and for some
of them the laws assign heavy and even the most extreme 12
penalties. But I will tell you what is the motive which
animates the present suit. It gives play to the malice of
a personal enemy, to his insolence, his abuse, his contumelies,

and every expression of his hostility : and yet, assuming that the charges and the imputations which have been made are true, it does not enable the State[n] to exact a penalty that is adequate, or nearly adequate, to the offences.

13 For it is not right to seek to debar another from coming before the people[n] and receiving a hearing, nor to do so in a spirit of malice and envy. Heaven knows, it is neither straightforward, nor citizen-like, nor just, men of Athens ! If the crimes by which he saw me injuring the city were of such a magnitude as he just now so theatrically set forth, he should have had recourse to the punishments enjoined by the laws at the time of the crimes themselves. If he saw me so acting as to deserve impeachment, he should have impeached me, and so brought me to trial before you ; if he saw me proposing illegal measures, he should have indicted me for their illegality. For surely, if he can prosecute Ctesiphon on my account, he would not have failed to indict me in person, had he thought that he could

14 convict me. And further, if he saw me committing any of those other crimes against you, which he just now slanderously enumerated, or any other crimes whatsoever, there are laws which deal with each, and punishments, and lawsuits and judgements involving penalties that are harsh and severe : to all of these he could have had recourse ; and from the moment when it was seen that he had acted so, and had conducted his hostilities against me on that plan, his present accusation of me would have been in line with his past

15 conduct. But as it is, he has forsaken the straight path of justice ; he has shrunk from all attempts to convict me at the time ; and after all these years, with the imputations, the jests, the invectives, that he has accumulated, he appears

to play his part. So it is, that though his accusations are against me, it is Ctesiphon that he prosecutes; and though he sets his quarrel with me in the forefront of the whole suit, he has never faced me in person to settle the quarrel, and it is another whom we see him trying to deprive of his civil rights. Yet surely, besides everything else that may be 16 pleaded on behalf of Ctesiphon, this, I think, may surely be most reasonably urged—that we ought in justice to have brought our own quarrel to the test by ourselves, instead of avoiding all conflict with one another, and looking for a third party to whom we could do harm. Such iniquity really passes all bounds.

From this one may see the nature of all his charges alike, 17 uttered, as they have been, without justice or regard for truth. Yet I desire also to examine them severally, and more particularly the false statements which he made against me in regard to the Peace and the Embassy, when he ascribed to me [n] the things which he himself had done in conjunction with Philocrates. And here it is necessary, men of Athens, and perhaps appropriate,[n] that I should remind you of the state of affairs subsisting during that period, so that you may view each group of actions in the light of the circumstances of the time.

When the Phocian war had broken out [n] (not through any 18 action of mine, for I had not yet entered public life), your own attitude, in the first place, was such, that you wished for the preservation of the Phocians, although you saw that their actions were unjustifiable; while you would have been delighted at anything that might happen to the Thebans, against whom you felt an indignation that was neither unreasonable nor unfair; for they had not used their good fortune at Leuctra with moderation. And, in the second place, the Peloponnese was all disunited : those who detested the Spartans [n] were not strong enough to annihilate them, and those who had previously governed with the support of Sparta [n] were no longer able to maintain their control over their cities ; but both these and all the other states were 19 in a condition of indeterminate strife and confusion. When Philip saw this (for it was not hard to see), he tried, by dispensing money to the traitors whom each state contained, to throw them all into collision and stir up one against another ; and thus, amid the blunders and perversity of others, he was making his own preparations, and growing great to the danger of all. And when it became clear to all that the then overbearing (but now unhappy) Thebans, distressed by the length of the war, would be forced to fly to you for aid,[n] Philip, to prevent this—to prevent the formation of any union between the cities—made offers of peace to you, and 20 of assistance to them. Now what was it that helped him, and enabled him to find in you his almost willing dupes ? It was the baseness (if that is the right name to use), or the ignorance, or both, of the rest of the Hellenes, who, though you were engaged in a long and continuous war, and that on behalf of the interests of all, as has been proved by the event, never assisted you either with money or with men, or in any other way whatsoever. And in your just and proper indignation with them, you listened readily to Philip. It was for these reasons, therefore, and not through any action of mine, that the Peace which we then conceded was negotiated ; and any one who investigates the matter honestly will find that it is the crimes and the corrupt practices of these men, in the course of the negotiations, that are responsible for our

position to-day. It is in the interests of truth that I enter 21
into all these events with this exactitude and thoroughness ;
for however strong the appearance of criminality in these
proceedings may be, it has, I imagine, nothing to do with
me. The first man to suggest or mention the Peace was
Aristodemus [n] the actor ; and the person who took the matter
up and moved the motion, and sold his services for the
purpose, along with Aeschines, was Philocrates of Hagnus—
your partner, Aeschines, not mine, even if you split your
sides with lying ; while those who supported him, from
whatever motive (for of that I say nothing at present), were
Eubulus and Cephisophon. I had no part in the matter
anywhere. And yet, although the facts are such as with 22
absolute truth I am representing them to be, he carried
his effrontery so far as to dare to assert that I was not
only responsible for the Peace, but had also prevented
the city from acting in conjunction with a general assembly
of the Hellenes in making it. What ? and you—oh !
how can one find a name that can be applied to you ?—
when you saw me (for you were there) preventing the city
from taking this great step and forming so grand an alliance
as you just now described, did you once raise a protest or
come forward to give information and to set forth the crimes
with which you now charge me ? If I had covenanted with 23
Philip for money that I would prevent the coalition of the
Hellenes, your only course was to refuse to keep silence—
to cry aloud, to protest, to reveal the fact to your fellow
countrymen. On no occasion did you do this : no such
utterance of yours was ever heard by any one. In fact there
was no embassy away at the time on a mission to any Hellenic
state ; the Hellenes had all long ago been tried and found

wanting; [n] and in all that he has said upon this matter there
24 is not a single sound word. And, apart from that, his falsehoods involve the greatest calumnies upon this city. For
if you were at one and the same time convoking the Hellenes
with a view to war, and sending ambassadors yourselves to
Philip to discuss peace, it was a deed for a Eurybatus,[n] not
a task for a state or for honest men, that you were carrying out.
But that is not the case ; indeed it is not. For what could
possibly have been your object in summoning them at that
moment ? Was it with a view to peace ? But they all had
peace already. Or with a view to war ? But you were
yourselves discussing peace. It is therefore evident that
neither was it I that introduced or was responsible for the
Peace in its original shape, nor is one of all the other falsehoods which he told of me shown to be true.

25　Again, consider the course of action which, when the city
had concluded the Peace, each of us now chose to adopt.
For from this you will know who it was that co-operated
with Philip throughout, and who it was that acted in your
interest and sought the good of the city. As for me, I proposed, as a member of the Council, that the ambassadors
should sail as quickly as possible to any district in which
they should ascertain Philip to be, and receive his oath from
26 him. But even when I had carried this resolution, they
would not act upon it. What did this mean, men of Athens ?
I will inform you. Philip's interest required that the interval
before he took the oath should be as long as possible ; yours,
that it should be as short as possible. And why ? Because
you broke off all your preparations for the war, not merely
from the day when he took the oath, but from the day
when you first hoped that Peace would be made ; and for

his part, this was what he was all along working for ; for he
thought (and with truth) that whatever places he could snatch
from Athens before he took the oath, would remain securely
his, since no one would break the Peace for their sake.   Fore- 27
seeing and calculating upon this, men of Athens, I proposed
this decree—that we should sail to any district in which
Philip might be, and receive his oath as soon as possible, in
order that the oaths might be taken while the Thracians,
your allies, were still in possession of those strongholds n of
which Aeschines just now spoke with contempt—Serrhium,
Myrtenum, and Ergiske ; and that Philip might not snatch
from us the keys of the country and make himself master
of Thrace, nor obtain an abundant supply of money and of
soldiers, and so proceed without difficulty to the prosecution
of his further designs.   And now, instead of citing or reading 28
this decree he slanders me on the ground that I thought
fit, as a member of the Council, to introduce the envoys.
But what should I have done ?   Was I to propose *not* to
introduce those who had come for the express purpose of
speaking with you ? or to order the lessee of the theatre
not to assign them seats ?   But they would have watched
the play from the threepenny seats,n if this decree had not
been proposed.   Should I have guarded the interests of the
city in petty details, and sold them wholesale, as my opponents did ?   Surely not.   (*To the clerk.*) Now take this decree,
which the prosecutor passed over, though he knew it well,
and read it.

> [*The decree of Demosthenes is read.*]   29

Though I had carried this decree, and was seeking the 30
good not of Philip, but of the city, these worthy ambassadors
paid little heed to it, but sat idle in Macedonia for three

whole months,[n] until Philip arrived from Thrace, after subduing the whole country; when they might, within ten days, or equally well[n] within three or four, have reached the Hellespont, and saved the strongholds, by receiving his oath before he could seize them. For he would not have touched them when we were present; or else, if he had done so, we should have refused to administer the oath to him; and in that case he would have failed to obtain the Peace: he would not have had both the Peace and the strongholds as well.

31   Such was Philip's first act of fraud, during the time of the Embassy, and the first instance of venality on the part of these wicked men; and over this I confess that then and now and always I have been and am at war and at variance with them. Now observe, immediately after
32 this, a second and even greater piece of villainy. As soon as Philip had sworn to the Peace, after first gaining possession of Thrace because these men did not obey my decree, he obtained from them—again by purchase—the postponement of our departure from Macedonia, until all should be in readiness for his campaign against the Phocians; in order that, instead of our bringing home a report of his intentions and his preparations for the march, which would make you set out and sail round to Thermopylae with your war-ships as you did before,[n] you might only hear our report of the facts when he was already on this side of Thermo-
33 pylae, and you could do nothing. And Philip was beset with such fear and such a weight of anxiety, lest in spite of his occupation of these places, his object should slip from his grasp, if, before the Phocians were destroyed, you resolved to assist them, that he hired this despicable creature, not

now in company with his colleagues, but by himself alone,
to make to you a statement and a report of such a character
that owing to them all was lost. But I request and entreat 34
you, men of Athens, to remember throughout this whole
trial, that, had Aeschines made no accusation that was not
included in the indictment, I too would not have said a word
that did not bear upon it ; but since he has had recourse
to all kinds of imputation and slander at once, I am
compelled also to give a brief answer to each group of
charges. What then were the statements uttered by him 35
that day, in consequence of which all was lost ? 'You must
not be perturbed,' he said, ' at Philip's having crossed to this
side of Thermopylae ; for you will get everything that you
desire, if you remain quiet ; and within two or three days
you will hear that he has become the friend of those whose
enemy he was, and the enemy of those whose friend he was,
when he first came. For,' said he, ' it is not phrases that
confirm friendships ' (a finely sententious expression !) ' but
identity of interest ; and it is to the interest of Philip and
of the Phocians and of yourselves alike, to be rid of the
heartless and overbearing demeanour of the Thebans.' To 36
these statements some gave a ready ear, in consequence of
the tacit ill-feeling towards the Thebans at the time. What
then followed—and not after a long interval, but immediately ?
The Phocians were overthrown ; their cities were razed to
the ground ; you, who had believed Aeschines and remained
inactive, were soon afterwards bringing in your effects from
the country ; while Aeschines received his gold ; and besides
all this, the city reaped the ill-will of the Thebans and Thessalians, while their gratitude for what had been done went
to Philip. To prove that this is so, (*to the clerk*) read me both 37

the decree of Callisthenes,[n] and Philip's letter. (*To the jury.*) These two documents together will make all the facts plain. (*To the clerk.*) Read.

38 [*The decree of Callisthenes is read.*]

Were these the hopes, on the strength of which you made the Peace? Was this what this hireling promised you? 39 (*To the clerk.*) Now read the letter which Philip sent after this.

[*Philip's letter is read.*]

40 You hear how obviously, in this letter sent to you, Philip is addressing definite information to his own allies. 'I have done these things,' he tells them, 'against the will of the Athenians, and to their annoyance; and so, men of Thebes and Thessaly, if you are wise, you will regard them as enemies, and will trust me.' He does not write in those actual terms, but that is what he intends to indicate. By these means he so carried them away, that they did not foresee or realize any of the consequences, but allowed him to get everything into his own power: and that is why, poor 41 men, they have experienced their present calamities. But the man who helped him to create this confidence, who co-operated with him, who brought home that false report and deluded you, he it is who now bewails the sufferings of the Thebans and enlarges upon their piteousness—he, who is himself the cause both of these and of the misery in Phocis, and of all the other evils which the Hellenes have endured. Yes, it is evident that you are pained at what has come to pass, Aeschines, and that you are sorry for the Thebans, when you have property in Boeotia[n] and are farming the land that was theirs; and that I rejoice at it—I, whose

surrender was immediately demanded by the author of the
disaster ! But I have digressed into subjects of which it 42
will perhaps be more convenient to speak presently. I will
return to the proofs which show that it is the crimes of
these men that are the cause of our condition to-day.

For when you had been deceived by Philip, through the
agency of these men, who while serving as ambassadors had
sold themselves and made a report in which there was not
a word of truth—when the unhappy Phocians had been
deceived and their cities annihilated—what followed ? The 43
despicable Thessalians and the slow-witted Thebans regarded
Philip as their friend, their benefactor, their saviour. Philip
was their all-in-all. They would not even listen to the
voice of any one who wished to express a different opinion.
You yourselves, though you viewed what had been done with
suspicion and vexation, nevertheless kept the Peace ; for
there was nothing else that you could have done. And the
other Hellenes, who, like yourselves, had been deluded and
disappointed of their hopes,[n] also kept the Peace, and gladly ;[n]
since in a sense they also were remotely aimed at by the war.
For when Philip was going about and subduing the Illyrians 44
and Triballi and some of the Hellenes as well, and bringing
many large forces into his own power, and when some of
the members of the several States were taking advantage
of the Peace to travel to Macedonia, and were being corrupted
—Aeschines among them—at such a time all of those whom
Philip had in view in thus making his preparations were
really being attacked by him. Whether they failed to realize 45
it is another question, which does not concern me. For I was
continually uttering warnings and protests, both in your
midst and wherever I was sent. But the cities were stricken

with disease : those who were engaged in political and practical affairs were taking bribes and being corrupted by the
hope of money ; while the mass of private citizens either
showed no foresight, or else were caught by the bait of
ease and leisure from day to day ; and all alike had fallen
victims to some such delusive fancy, as that the danger
would come upon every one but themselves, and that
through the perils of others they would be able to secure
46 their own position as they pleased. And so, I suppose, it
has come to pass that the masses have atoned for their great
and ill-timed indifference by the loss of their freedom, while
the leaders in affairs, who fancied that they were selling
everything except themselves, have realized that they had
sold themselves first of all. For instead of being called friends
and guest-friends, as they were called at the time when they
were taking their bribes, they now hear themselves called
flatterers, and god-forsaken, and all the other names that
47 they deserve. For no one, men of Athens, spends his money
out of a desire to benefit the traitor ; nor, when once he
has secured the object for which he bargains, does he employ
the traitor to advise him with regard to other objects : if it
were so, nothing could be happier than a traitor. But it is
not so, of course. Far from it! When the aspirant after
dominion has gained his object, he is also the master of those
who have sold it to him : and because then he knows their
villainy, he then hates and mistrusts them, and covers them
48 with insults. For observe—for even if the time of the events
is past, the time for realizing truths like these is ever present
to wise men. Lasthenes [n] was called his 'friend'; but only
until he had betrayed Olynthus. And Timolaus ; [n] but only
until he had destroyed Thebes. And Eudicus and Simus [n]

of Larissa ; but only until they had put Thessaly in Philip's power. And now, persecuted as they are, and insulted, and subjected to every kind of misery, the whole inhabited world has become filled with such men. And what of Aristratus[n] at Sicyon ? what of Perillus[n] at Megara ? Are they not outcasts ? From these instances one can see very clearly, that it is he who 49 best protects his own country and speaks most constantly against such men, that secures for traitors and hirelings like yourselves, Aeschines, the continuance of your opportunities for taking bribes. It is the majority of those who are here, those who resist your will, that you must thank for the fact that you live and draw your pay ; for, left to yourselves, you would long ago have perished.

There is still much that I might say about the transactions 50 of that time, but I think that even what I have said is more than enough. The blame rests with Aeschines, who has drenched me with the stale dregs[n] of his own villainy and crime, from which I was compelled to clear myself in the eyes of those who are too young to remember the events ; though perhaps you who knew, even before I said a single word, of Aeschines' service as a hireling, may have felt some annoyance as you listened. He calls it, forsooth, 'friendship' 51 and 'guest-friendship' ; and somewhere in his speech just now he used the expression, ' the man who casts in my teeth my guest-friendship with Alexander.' *I* cast in your teeth your guest-friendship with Alexander ? How did you acquire it ? How came you to be thought worthy of it ? Never would I call you the guest-friend of Philip or the friend of Alexander —I am not so insane—unless you are to call harvesters and other hired servants the friends and guest-friends of those who have hired them. [But that is not the case, of course. Far from it !] Nay, I call you the hireling, formerly 52

of Philip, and now of Alexander, and so do all who are present.
If you disbelieve me, ask them—or rather I will ask them for
you. Men of Athens, do you think of Aeschines as the hireling
or as the guest-friend of Alexander? You hear what they say.

53   I now wish, without more delay, to make my defence
upon the indictment itself, and to go through my past
acts, in order that Aeschines may hear (though he knows
them well) the grounds on which I claim to have a right
both to the gifts which the Council have proposed, and
even to far greater than these. (*To the clerk.*) Now take
the indictment and read it.

54, 55   [*The indictment is read.*]

56   These, men of Athens, are the points in the resolution
which the prosecutor assails; and these very points will,
I think, afford me my first means of proving to you that the
defence which I am about to offer is an absolutely fair one.
For I will take the points of the indictment in the very same
order as the prosecutor: I will speak of each in succession,
57 and will knowingly pass over nothing. Any decision upon
the statement that I 'consistently do and say what is best
for the People, and am eager to do whatever good I can',
and upon the proposal to vote me thanks for this, depends,
I consider, upon my past political career: for it is by an
investigation of my career that either the truth and the
propriety, or else the falsehood, of these statements which
58 Ctesiphon has made about me will be discovered. Again,
the proposal to crown me, without the addition of the
clause 'when he has submitted to his examination',
and the order to proclaim the award of the crown in the
theatre, must, I imagine, stand or fall with my political

career; for the question is whether I deserve the crown and the proclamation before my fellow countrymen or not. At the same time I consider myself further bound to point out to you the laws under which the defendant's proposal could be made. In this honest and straightforward manner, men of Athens, I have determined to make my defence; and now I will proceed to speak of my past actions themselves. And let no one imagine that I am detaching 59 my argument from its connexion with the indictment, if I break into a discussion of international transactions. For it is the prosecutor who, by assailing the clause of the decree which states that I do and say what is best, and by indicting it as false, has rendered the discussion of my whole political career essentially germane to the indictment; and further, out of the many careers which public life offers, it was the department of international affairs that I chose; so that I have a right to derive my proofs also from that department.

I will pass over all that Philip snatched from us and 60 secured, in the days before I took part in public life as an orator. None of these losses, I imagine, has anything to do with me. But I will recall to you, and will render you an account of all that, from the day when I entered upon this career, he was *prevented* from taking, when I have made one remark. Philip, men of Athens, had a great advantage 61 in his favour. For in the midst of the Hellenic peoples—and not of some only, but of all alike—there had sprung up a crop of traitors—corrupt, god-forsaken men—more numerous than they have ever been within the memory of man. These he took to help and co-operate with him; and great as the mutual ill-will and dissensions of the Hellenes already were, he rendered them even worse, by deceiving some, making presents to others, and corrupting others in every way; and at a time when all had in reality but one interest—to prevent his becoming powerful—he divided

62 them into a number of factions. All the Hellenes then being in this condition, still ignorant of the growing and accumulating evil, you have to ask yourselves, men of Athens, what policy and action it was fitting for the city to choose, and to hold me responsible for this; for the person who assumed that responsibility in the State was

63 myself. Should she, Aeschines, have sacrificed her pride and her own dignity? Should she have joined the ranks of the Thessalians and Dolopes,[n] and helped Philip to acquire the empire of Hellas, cancelling thereby the noble and righteous deeds of our forefathers? Or, if she should not have done this (for it would have been in very truth an atrocious thing), should she have looked on, while all that she saw would happen, if no one prevented it—all that she realized, it seems,

64 at a distance—was actually taking place? Nay, I should be glad to ask to-day the severest critic of my actions, which party he would have desired the city to join—the party which shares the responsibility for the misery and disgrace which has fallen upon the Hellenes (the party of the Thessalians and their supporters, one may call it), or the party which looked on while these calamities were taking place, in the hope of gaining some advantage for themselves—in which we should place the Arcadians and Messenians and

65 Argives. But even of these, many—nay, all—have in the end fared worse than we. For if Philip had departed immediately after his victory, and gone his way; if afterwards he had remained at peace, and had given no trouble whatever to

any of his own allies or of the other Hellenes ; then there would have been some ground for blaming and accusing those who had opposed his plans. But if he has stripped them all alike of their dignity, their paramountcy, and their independence—nay, even of their free constitutions,[n] wherever he could do so—can it be denied that the policy which you adopted on my advice was the most glorious policy possible ?

But I return to my former point. What was it fitting for 66 the city to do, Aeschines, when she saw Philip establishing for himself a despotic sway over the Hellenes ? What language should have been used, what measures proposed, by the adviser of the people at Athens (for that it was at Athens makes the utmost difference), when I knew that from the very first, up to the day when I myself ascended the platform, my country had always contended for pre-eminence, honour, and glory, and in the cause of honour, and for the interests of all, had sacrificed more money and lives than any other Hellenic people had spent for their private ends : when 67 I saw that Philip himself, with whom our conflict lay, for the sake of empire and absolute power, had had his eye knocked out, his collar-bone broken, his hand and his leg maimed, and was ready to resign any part of his body that Fortune chose to take from him, provided that with what remained he might live in honour and glory ? And surely no one would 68 dare to say that it was fitting that in one bred at Pella, a place then inglorious and insignificant, there should have grown up so lofty a spirit that he aspired after the empire of Hellas, and conceived such a project in his mind ; but that in you, who are Athenians, and who day by day in all that you hear and see behold the memorials of the gallantry

of your forefathers, such baseness should be found, that you
would yield up your liberty to Philip by your own deliberate
69 offer and deed. No man would say this. One alternative
remained, and that, one which you were bound to take—
that of a righteous resistance to the whole course of action
by which he was doing you injury. You acted thus from the
first, quite rightly and properly ; while I helped by my proposals and advice during the time of my political activity,
and I do not deny it. But what ought I to have done ? For
the time has come to ask you this, Aeschines, and to dis-
70 miss everything else. Amphipolis, Pydna, Poteidaea, Halonnesus—all are blotted from my memory. As for Serrhium,
Doriscus, the sack of Peparethus, and all the other injuries
inflicted upon the city, I renounce all knowledge of their ever
having happened—though you actually said that *I* involved
my countrymen in hostility by talking of these things, when
the decrees which deal with them were the work of Eubulus
and Aristophon [n] and Diopeithes,[n] and not mine at all—so
71 glibly do you assert anything that suits your purpose ! But
of this too I say nothing at present. I only ask you whether
Philip, who was appropriating Euboea,[n] and establishing it
as a stronghold to command Attica ; who was making an
attempt upon Megara, seizing Oreus, razing the walls of
Porthmus, setting up Philistides as tyrant at Oreus and
Cleitarchus at Eretria, bringing the Hellespont into his
own power, besieging Byzantium, destroying some of the
cities of Hellas, and restoring his exiled friends to others—
whether he, I say, in acting thus, was guilty of wrong,
violating the truce and breaking the Peace, or not ? Was it
fit that one of the Hellenes should arise to prevent it, or not ?
72 If it was not fit—if it was fit that Hellas should become like

the Mysian booty [n] in the proverb before men's eyes, while
the Athenians had life and being, then I have lost my labour
in speaking upon this theme, and the city has lost its labour
in obeying me : then let everything that has been done be
counted for a crime and a blunder, and those my own ! But
if it was right that one should arise to prevent it, for whom
could the task be more fitting than for the people of Athens ?
That then, was the aim of *my* policy ; and when I saw Philip
reducing all mankind to servitude, I opposed him, and without
ceasing warned and exhorted you to make no surrender.

But the Peace, Aeschines, was in reality broken by Philip, 73
when he seized the corn-ships, not by Athens. (*To the
clerk*.) Bring the decrees themselves, and the letter of
Philip, and read them in order. (*To the jury*.) For they
will make it clear who is responsible, and for what.

[*A decree is read.*]   74

This decree then was proposed by Eubulus, not by me ; 75
and the next by Aristophon ; he is followed first by Hegesippus, and he by Aristophon again, and then by Philocrates,
then by Cephisophon, and then by all of them. But I
proposed no decree upon this subject. (*To the clerk*.) Read.

[*Decrees are read.*]

As then I point to these decrees, so, Aeschines, do you 76
point to a decree of any kind, proposed by me, which makes
me responsible for the war. You cannot do so : for had you
been able, there is nothing which you would sooner have
produced. Indeed, even Philip himself makes no charge
against me as regards the war, though he complains of
others. (*To the clerk*.) Read Philip's letter itself.

[*Philip's letter is read.*]

79   In this letter he has nowhere mentioned the name of Demosthenes, nor made any charge against me. Why is it then that, though he complains of others, he has not mentioned my own actions? Because, if he had written anything about me, he must have mentioned his own acts of wrong; for it was these acts upon which I kept my grip, and these which I opposed. First of all, when he was trying to steal into the Peloponnese, I proposed the embassy to the Peloponnese;[n] then, when he was grasping at Euboea, the embassy to Euboea;[n] then the expedition—not an embassy any more—to Oreus,[n] and that to Eretria, when he had established

80 tyrants in those cities. After that I dispatched all the naval expeditions, in the course of which the Chersonese and Byzantium and all our allies were saved. In consequence of this, the noblest rewards at the hands of those who had benefited by your action became yours—votes of thanks, glory, honours, crowns, gratitude; while of the victims of his aggression, those who followed your advice at the time secured their own deliverance, and those who neglected it had the memory of your warnings constantly in their minds, and regarded you not merely as their well-wishers, but as men of wisdom and prophetic insight; for

81 all that you foretold has come to pass. And further, that Philistides would have given a large sum to retain Oreus, and Cleitarchus to retain Eretria, and Philip himself, to be able to count upon the use of these places against you, and to escape all exposure of his other proceedings and all investigation, by any one in any place, of his wrongful acts—all this is not unknown to any one, least of all to you, Aeschines.

For the envoys sent at that time by Cleitarchus and Phili- 82 stides lodged at your house, when they came here, and you acted as their patron.[n] Though the city rejected them, as enemies whose proposals were neither just nor expedient, to you they were friends. None of their attempts succeeded, slander me though you may, when you assert that I say nothing when I receive money, but cry out when I spend it. That, certainly, is not *your* way : for you cry out with money in your hands, and will never cease, unless those present cause you to do so by taking away your civil rights [n] to-day. Now on that occasion, gentlemen, you crowned me for my 83 conduct. Aristonicus proposed a decree whose very syllables were identical with those of Ctesiphon's present proposal ; the crown was proclaimed in the theatre ; and this was already the second proclamation [n] in my honour : and yet Aeschines, though he was there, neither opposed the decree, nor indicted the mover. (*To the clerk.*) Take this decree also and read it.

[*The decree of Aristonicus is read.*]   84

Now is any of you aware of any discredit that attached 85 itself to the city owing to this decree ? Did any mockery or ridicule ensue, such as Aeschines said must follow on the present occasion, if I were crowned ? But surely when proceedings are recent and well known to all, then it is that, if they are satisfactory, they meet with gratitude, and if they are otherwise, with punishment. It appears, then, that on that occasion I met with gratitude, not with blame or punishment.

Thus the fact that, up to the time when these events took 86 place, I acted throughout as was best for the city, has been acknowledged by the victory of my advice and my proposals in your deliberations, by the successful execution of the measures which I proposed, and the award of crowns in consequence of them to the city and to myself and to all, and by your celebration of sacrifices to the gods, and processions, in thankfulness for these blessings.

87   When Philip had been expelled from Euboea—and while the arms which expelled him were yours, the statesmanship and the decrees (even though some of my opponents may split their sides) were mine—he proceeded to look for some other stronghold from which he could threaten the city. And seeing that we were more dependent than any other people upon imported corn, and wishing to get our corn-trade into his power, he advanced to Thrace. First, he requested the Byzantines, his own allies, to join him in the war against you ; and when they refused and said (with truth) that they had not made their alliance with him for such a purpose, he erected a stockade against the city, brought up his engines,

88 and proceeded to besiege it. I will not ask again what you ought to have done when this was happening ; it is manifest to all. But who was it that went to the rescue of the Byzantines, and saved them ? Who was it that prevented the Hellespont from falling into other hands at that time ? It was you, men of Athens—and when I say ' you ', I mean this city. And who was it that spoke and moved resolutions and acted for the city, and gave himself up unsparingly to

89 the business of the State ? It was I. But of the immense benefit thus conferred upon all, you no longer need words of mine to tell you, since you have had actual experience of it. For the war which then ensued, apart from the glorious reputation that it brought you, kept you supplied

with the necessaries of life in greater plenty and at lower
prices than the present Peace, which these worthy men are
guarding to their country's detriment, in their hopes of
something yet to be realized. May those hopes be disappointed ! May they share the fortune which you, who wish
for the best, ask of the gods, rather than cause you to share
that upon which their own choice is fixed ! (*To the clerk.*)
Read out to the jury the crowns awarded to the city in
consequence of her action by the Byzantines and by the
Perinthians.

[*The decree of the Byzantines is read.*]   90, 91

Read out also the crowns awarded by the peoples of the 92
Chersonese.

[*The decree of the peoples of the Chersonese is read.*]

Thus the policy which I had adopted was not only success- 93
ful in saving the Chersonese and Byzantium, in preventing
the Hellespont from falling at that time into the power of
Philip, and in bringing honours to the city in consequence,
but it revealed to the whole world the noble gallantry of
Athens and the baseness of Philip. For all saw that he, the
ally of the Byzantines, was besieging them—what could be
more shameful or revolting ? and on the other hand, it was 94
seen that you, who might fairly have urged many well-
founded complaints against them for their inconsiderate
conduct [n] towards you at an earlier period, not only refused
to remember your grudge and to abandon the victims of
aggression, but actually delivered them ; and in consequence
of this, you won glory and goodwill on all hands. And
further, though every one knows that you have crowned
many public men before now, no one can name any but

myself—that is to say, any public counsellor and orator—
for whose merits the city has received a crown.

95   In order to prove to you, also, that the slanders which he
uttered against the Euboeans and Byzantines, as he recalled
to you any ill-natured action that they had taken towards
you in the past, are disingenuous calumnies, not only because
they are false (for this, I think, you may all be assumed to
know), but also because, however true they might be, it was
still to your advantage to deal with the political situation
as I have done, I desire to describe, and that briefly, one or
two of the noble deeds which this city has done in your own
time. For an individual and a State should strive always,
in their respective spheres, to fashion their future conduct
96 after the highest examples that their past affords. Thus,
men of Athens, at a time when the Spartans were masters
of land and sea,[n] and were retaining their hold, by means
of governors and garrisons, upon the country all round
Attica—Euboea, Tanagra, all Boeotia, Megara, Aegina, Ceos,
and the other islands—and when Athens possessed neither
ships nor walls, you marched forth to Haliartus, and again,
not many days later, to Corinth, though the Athenians of
that day might have borne a heavy grudge against both the
Corinthians and the Thebans for the part they had played
97 in reference to the Deceleian War.[n] But they bore no such
grudge. Far from it! And neither of these actions, Aeschines,
was taken by them to help benefactors; nor was the prospect
before them free from danger. Yet they did not on that
account sacrifice those who fled to them for help. For
the sake of glory and honour they were willing to expose
themselves to the danger; and it was a right and a noble
spirit that inspired their counsels. For the life of all men

must end in death, though a man shut himself in a chamber
and keep watch ; but brave men must ever set themselves
to do that which is noble, with their joyful hope for their
buckler, and whatsoever God gives, must bear it gallantly.
Thus did your forefathers, and thus did the elder among 98
yourselves : for, although the Spartans were no friends or
benefactors of yours, but had done much grievous wrong to
the city, yet, when the Thebans, after their victory at
Leuctra, attempted to annihilate them, you prevented it,
not terrified by the strength or the reputation which the
Thebans then enjoyed, nor reckoning up what the men had
done to you, for whom you were to face this peril. And 99
thus, as you know, you revealed to all the Hellenes, that whatever offences may be committed against you, though under
all other circumstances you show your resentment of them,
yet if any danger to life or freedom overtakes the trans-
gressors, you will bear no grudge and make no reckoning.
Nor was it in these instances only that you were thus disposed.
For once more, when the Thebans were appropriating
Euboea,[n] you did not look on while it was done ; you did
not call to mind the wrong which had been done to you
in the matter of Oropus[n] by Themison and Theodorus :
you helped even these ; and it was then that the city for
the first time had voluntary trierarchs, of whom I was one.[n]
But I will not speak of this yet. And although to save the 100
island was itself a noble thing to do, it was a yet nobler
thing by far, that when their lives and their cities were
absolutely in your power, you gave them back, as it was right
to do, to the very men who had offended against you, and
made no reckoning, when such trust had been placed in you,
of the wrongs which you had suffered. I pass by the innumer-

able instances which I might still give—battles at sea, expeditions [by land, campaigns] both long ago and now in our day ; in all of which the object of the city has been to defend
101 the freedom and safety of the other Hellenic peoples. And so, when in all these striking examples I had beheld the city ever ready to strive in defence of the interests of others, what was I likely to bid her do, what action was I likely to recommend to her, when the debate to some extent concerned her own interests ? 'Why,' you would say, 'to remember her grudge against those who wanted deliverance, and to look for excuses for sacrificing everything ! ' And who would not have been justified in putting me to death, if I had attempted to bring shame upon the city's high traditions, though it were only by word ? The deed itself you would never have done, I know full well; for had you desired to do it, what was there to hinder you ? Were you not free so to act ? Had you not these men here to propose it ?

102 I wish now to return to the next in succession of my political acts ; and here again you must ask yourselves, what was the best thing for the city ? For, men of Athens, when I saw that your navy was breaking up, and that, while the rich were obtaining exemption on the strength of small payments,[n] citizens of moderate or small means were losing all that they had ; and further, that in consequence of these things the city was always missing her opportunities ; I enacted a law in accordance with which I compelled the former—the rich— to do their duty fairly ; I put an end to the injustice done to the poor, and (what was the greatest service of all to the
103 State) I caused our preparations to be made in time. When I was indicted for this, I appeared before you at the ensuing

trial, and was acquitted ; the prosecutor failed to obtain
the necessary fraction of the votes. But what sums do you
think the leaders of the Taxation-Boards, or those who
stood second or third, offered me, to induce me, if possible,
not to enact the law, or at least to let it drop and lie under
sworn notice of prosecution ? [n] They offered sums so large,
men of Athens, that I should hesitate to mention them to you.
It was a natural course for them to take. For under the 104
former laws it was possible for them to divide their obligation
between sixteen persons, paying little or nothing themselves,
and grinding down their poorer fellow citizens : while by
my law each must pay down a sum calculated in proportion
to his property ; and a man came to be charged with two
warships, who had previously been one of sixteen subscribers
to a single one (for they used now to call themselves no
longer captains of their ships, but subscribers). Thus there
was nothing that they were not willing to give, if only the
new plan could be brought to nothing, and they could escape
being compelled to do their duty fairly. (*To the clerk.*)
Now read me, first, the decree [n] in accordance with which 105
I had to meet the indictment ; and then the lists of those
liable under the former law, and under my own, respectively.
Read.

[*The decree is read.*]

Now produce that noble list.   106

[*A list is read.*]

Now produce, for comparison with this, the list under
my own law.

[*A list is read.*]

Was this, think you, but a trifling assistance which I rendered
107 to the poor among you ? Would the wealthy have spent but a
trifling sum to avoid doing their duty fairly ? I am proud not
only of having refused all compromise upon the measure, not
only of having been acquitted when I was indicted, but also
of having enacted a law which was beneficial, and of having
given proof of it in practice. For throughout the war the
armaments were equipped under my law, and no trierarch
ever laid the suppliants' branch [n] before you in token of
grievance, nor took sanctuary at Munychia; none was
imprisoned by the Admiralty Board; no warship was
abandoned at sea and lost to the State, or left behind here
as unseaworthy. Under the former laws all these things
108 used to happen; and the reason was that the obligation
rested upon the poor, and in consequence there were many
cases of inability to discharge it. I transferred the duties
of the trierarchy from the poor to the rich; and therefore
every duty was properly fulfilled. Aye, and for this very
reason I deserve to receive praise—that I always adopted
such political measures as brought with them accessions of
glory and honour and power to the city. No measure of
mine is malicious, harsh, or unprincipled; none is degrading
or unworthy of the city. The same spirit will be seen both
109 in my domestic and my international policy. For just as
in home affairs I did not set the favour of the rich above
the rights of the many, so in international affairs I did not
embrace the gifts and the friendship of Philip, in preference
to the common interests of all the Hellenes.

It still remains for me, I suppose, to speak about the pro-
110 clamation, and about my examination. The statement that
I acted for the best, and that I am loyal to you throughout

and eager to do you good service, I have proved, I think,
sufficiently, by what I have said. At the same time I am
passing over the most important parts of my political life
and actions; for I conceive that I ought first to render
to you in their proper order my arguments in regard
to the alleged illegality itself: which done, even if I say
nothing about the rest of my political acts, I can still rely
upon that personal knowledge of them which each of you
possesses.

Of the arguments which the prosecutor jumbled together
in utter confusion with reference to the laws accompanying 111
his indictment,[n] I am quite certain that you could not
follow the greater part, nor could I understand them myself;
but I will simply address you straightforwardly upon the
question of right. So far am I from claiming (as he just
now slanderously declared) to be free from the liability to
render an account, that I admit a life-long liability to account
for every part of my administration and policy. But I do 112
not admit that I am liable for one single day—you hear me,
Aeschines?—to account for what I have given to the People
as a free-will offering out of my private estate; nor is
any one else so liable, not even if he is one of the nine
archons. What law is so replete with injustice and chur-
lishness, that when a man has made a present out of his
private property and done an act of generosity and munificence, it deprives him of the gratitude due to him, hales him
before a court of disingenuous critics, and sets them to audit
accounts of sums which he himself has given? There is
no such law. If the prosecutor asserts that there is, let him
produce it, and I will resign myself and say no more. But 113
the law does not exist, men of Athens; this is nothing but

an informer's trick on the part of Aeschines, who, because I was Controller of the Festival Fund when I made this donation, says, ' Ctesiphon proposed a vote of thanks to him when he was still liable to account.' The vote of thanks was not for any of the things for which I was liable to account ; it was for my voluntary gift, and your charge is a mis-representation. ' Yes,' you say, ' but you were also a Com-missioner of Fortifications.' I was, and thanks were rightly accorded me on the very ground that, instead of charging the sums which I spent, I made a present of them. A statement of account, it is true, calls for an audit and scrutineers ; but a free gift deserves gratitude and thanks ; and that is why the defendant proposed this motion in my favour.

114 That this principle is not merely laid down in the laws, but rooted in your national character, I shall have no difficulty in proving by many instances. Nausicles,[n] to begin with, has often been crowned by you, while general, for sacrifices which he had made from his private funds. Again, when Diotimus[n] gave the shields, and Charidemus[n] afterwards, they were crowned. And again, Neoptolemus here, while still director of many public works, has received honours for his voluntary gifts. It would really be too bad, if any one who held any office must either be debarred thereby from making a present to the State, or else, instead of receiving due gratitude, must submit accounts of the sums given.

115 To prove the truth of my statements, (*to the clerk*) take and read the actual decrees which were passed in honour of these persons. Read.

116   [*Two decrees are read.*]

117   Each of these persons, Aeschines, was accountable as regards the office which he held, but not as regards the services for

which he was crowned. Nor am I, therefore ; for I presume
that I have the same rights as others with reference to the
same matters. I made a voluntary gift. For this I receive
thanks ; for I am not liable to account for what I gave. I was
holding office. True, and I have rendered an account of
my official expenditure, but not of what I gave voluntarily.
Ah ! but I exercised my office iniquitously ! What ? and
you were there, when the auditors brought me before them,
and did not accuse me ?

Now that the court may see that the prosecutor himself **118**
bears me witness that I was crowned for services of which
I was not liable to render an account, (*to the clerk*) take
and read the decree which was proposed in my honour,
in its entirety. (*To the jury.*) The points which he has
omitted to indict in the Council's resolution will show that
the charges which he does make are deliberate misrepresentations. (*To the clerk.*)   Read.

[*The decree is read.*]

My donations then, were these, of which you have not **119**
made one the subject of indictment. It is the reward for
these, which the Council states to be my due, that you
attack. You admit that it was legal to accept the gifts
offered, and you indict as illegal the return of gratitude for
them. In Heaven's name, what must the perfect scoundrel,
the really heaven-detested, malignant being be like ? Must
he not be a man like this ?

But as regards the proclamation in the theatre, I pass by **120**
the fact that ten thousand persons have been thus proclaimed
on ten thousand different occasions, and that my own name
has often been so proclaimed before. But, in Heaven's name,

Aeschines, are you so perverse and stupid, that you cannot
grasp the fact that the recipient of the crown feels the same
pride wherever the crown is proclaimed, and that it is for
the benefit of those who confer it that the proclamation is
made in the theatre ?   For those who hear are stimulated
to do good service to the State, and commend those who
return gratitude for such service even more than they
commend the recipient of the crown.   That is why the city
has enacted this law. (*To the clerk.*)   Take the law itself
and read it.

[The law is read.]

121   Do you hear, Aeschines, the plain words of the law ?
' Except such as the People or the Council shall resolve so
to proclaim.   But let these be proclaimed.'   Why, wretched
man, do you lay this dishonest charge ?   Why do you invent
false arguments ?   Why do you not take hellebore [n] to cure
you ?   What ?   Are you not ashamed to bring a case founded
upon envy, not upon any crime—to alter some of the laws,
and to leave out parts of others, when they ought surely, in
justice, to be read entire to those who have sworn to give
122 their votes in accordance with the laws ?   And then, while
you act in this way, you enumerate the qualities which should
be found in a friend of the People, as if you had contracted
for a statue, and discovered on receiving it that it had not
the features required by the contract ; or as if a friend of
the People was known by a definition, and not by his works
and his political measures !   And you shout out expressions,
proper and improper, like a reveller on a cart [n]—expressions
which apply to you and your house, not to me.   I will add
123 this also, men of Athens.   The difference between abuse and
accusation is, I imagine, that an accusation is founded upon

crimes, for which the penalties are assigned by law ; abuse, upon such slanders as their own character leads enemies to utter about one another. And I conceive that our forefathers built these courts of law, not that we might assemble you here and revile one another with improper expressions suggested by our adversary's private life, but that we might convict any one who happens to have committed some crime against the State. Aeschines knew this as well as I ; 124 and yet he chose to make a ribald attack instead of an accusation. At the same time, it is not fair that he should go off without getting as much as he gives, even in this respect ; and when I have asked him one question, I will at once proceed to the attack. Are we to call you, Aeschines, the enemy of the State, or of myself ? Of myself, of course. What ? And when you might have exacted the penalty from me, on behalf of your fellow countrymen, according to the laws— at public examinations, by indictment, by all other forms of trial—did you always omit to do so ? And yet to-day, 125 when I am unassailable upon every ground—on the ground of law, of lapse of time, of the statutable limit,[n] of the many previous trials which I have undergone upon every charge, without having once been convicted of any crime against you to this day—and when the city must necessarily share to a greater or smaller degree in the glory of acts which were really acts of the people, have you confronted me upon such an issue as this ? Take care lest, while you profess to be *my* enemy, you prove to be the enemy of your fellow countrymen !

Since then I have shown you all what is the vote which 126 religion and justice demand of you, I am now obliged, it would seem, by the slanders which he has uttered (though

I am no lover of abuse) to reply to his many falsehoods by
saying just what is absolutely necessary about himself, and
showing who he is, and whence he is sprung, that he so lightly
begins to use bad language, pulling to pieces certain expressions of mine, when he has himself used expressions which

127 any respectable man would have shrunk from uttering ; for
if the accuser were Aeacus or Rhadamanthus or Minos,[n]
instead of a scandal-monger,[n] an old hand in the market-
place,[n] a pestilent clerk, I do not believe that he would
have spoken thus, or produced such a stock of ponderous
phrases, crying aloud, as if he were acting a tragedy, ' O Earth
and Sun and Virtue,'[n] and the like ; or again, invoking
' Wit and Culture, by which things noble and base are dis-
cerned apart '—for, of course, you heard him speaking

128 in this way. Scum of the earth ! What have you or yours
to do with virtue ? How should *you* discern what is noble
and what is not ? Where and how did you get your qualification to do so ? What right have *you* to mention culture
anywhere ? A man of genuine culture would not only never
have asserted such a thing of himself, but would have blushed
to hear another do so : and those who, like you, fall far short
of it, but are tactless enough to claim it, succeed only in
causing distress to their hearers, when they speak—not in
seeming to be what they profess.

129 But though I am not at a loss to know what to say about
you and yours, I am at a loss to know what to mention first.
Shall I tell first [n] how your father Tromes was a slave in the
house of Elpias, who kept an elementary school near the
temple of Theseus, and how he wore shackles and a wooden
halter ? Or how your mother, by celebrating her daylight
nuptials in her hut near the shrine of the Hero of the Lancet,[n]

was enabled to rear you, her beautiful statue, the prince of
third-rate actors ?   But these things are known to all without
my telling them.   Shall I tell how Phormio, the ship's piper,
the slave of Dion of Phrearrii, raised her up out of this noble
profession ?   But, before God and every Heavenly Power,
I shudder lest in using expressions which are fitly applied
to you, I may be thought to have chosen a subject upon
which it ill befits myself to speak.   So I will pass this by, 130
and will begin with the acts of his own life ; for they were
not like any chance actions,[n] but such as the people curses.
For only lately—lately, do I say ? only yesterday or the day
before—did he become at once an Athenian and an orator,
and by the addition of two syllables converted his father from
Tromes into Atrometus, and gave his mother the imposing
name of Glaucothea,[n] when every one knows that she used
to be called Empusa [n]—a name which was obviously given
her because there was nothing that she would not do or have
done to her ; for how else should she have acquired it ?   Yet, 131
in spite of this, you are of so ungrateful and villainous a
nature, that though, thanks to your countrymen, you have
risen from slavery to freedom, and from poverty to wealth,
far from feeling gratitude to them, you devote your political
activity to working against them as a hireling.   I will pass
over every case in which there is any room for the contention
that he has spoken in the interests of the city, and will
remind you of the acts which he was manifestly proved to
have done for the good of her enemies.

Which of you has not heard of Antiphon,[n] who was struck 132
off the list of citizens,[n] and came into the city in pursuance
of a promise to Philip that he would burn the dockyards ?
I found him concealed in the Peiraeus, and brought him

before the Assembly ; but the malignant Aeschines shouted
at the top of his voice, that it was atrocious of me, in a
democratic country, to insult a citizen who had met with
misfortune, and to go to men's houses without a decree; [n]
133 and he obtained his release. And unless the Council of
Areopagus had taken notice of the matter, and, seeing the
inopportuneness of the ignorance which you had shown,
had made a further search for the man, and arrested
him, and brought him before you again, a man of that
character would have been snatched out of your hands, and
would have evaded punishment, and been sent out of the
country by this pompous orator. As it was, you tortured
and executed him—and so ought you also to have treated
134 Aeschines. The Council of Areopagus knew the part which
he had played in this affair ; and for this reason, when, owing
to the same ignorance which so often leads you to sacrifice
the public interests, you elected him [n] to advocate your
claims in regard to the Temple of Delos, the Council (since
you had appointed it to assist you and entrusted it with
full authority to act in the matter) immediately rejected
Aeschines as a traitor, and committed the case to Hypereides.
When the Council took this step, the members took their
votes from the altar,[n] and not one vote was given for this
135 abominable man. To prove that what I say is true, (*to the
clerk*) call the witnesses who testify to it.

[*The witnesses are called.*]

136   Thus when the Council rejected him from the office of
advocate, and committed the case to another, it declared
at the same time that he was a traitor, who wished you ill.

Such was one of the public appearances of this fine fellow,

and such its character—so like the acts with which he charges
me, is it not ? Now recall a second. For when Philip sent
Python of Byzantium,[n] and with him envoys from all his
allies, in the hope of putting the city to shame and showing
her to be in the wrong, I would not give way before the
torrent of insolent rhetoric which Python poured out upon
you, but rose and contradicted him, and would not betray
the city's rights, but proved the iniquity of Philip's actions
so manifestly, that even his own allies rose up and admitted
it. But Aeschines supported Python ; he gave testimony in
opposition to his country, and that testimony false.

Nor was this sufficient for him ; for again after this he **137**
was detected going to meet Anaxinus [n] the spy in the house
of Thrason. But surely one who met the emissary of the
enemy alone and conferred with him, must himself have
been already a born spy and an enemy of his country. To
prove the truth of what I say, (*to the clerk*) call the witnesses
to these facts.

[*The witnesses are called.*]

There are still an infinite number of things which I might **138**
relate of him ; but I pass them over. For the truth is
something like this. I could still point to many instances in
which he was found to be serving our enemies during that
period, and showing his spite against me. But you do not
store such things up in careful remembrance, to visit them
with the indignation which they deserve ; but, following
a bad custom, you have given great freedom to any one
who wishes to trip up the proposer of any advantageous
measure by dishonest charges—bartering, as you do, the
advantage of the State for the pleasure and gratification which

you derive from invective; and so it is always easier and safer to be a hireling in the service of the enemy, than a statesman who has chosen to defend your cause.

139   To co-operate with Philip before we were openly at war with him was—I call Earth and Heaven to witness—atrocious enough.   How could it be otherwise—against his own country?   Nevertheless, concede him this, if you will, concede him this.   But when the corn-ships had been openly plundered, and the Chersonese was being ravaged, and the man was on the march against Attica; when the position of affairs was no longer in doubt, and war had begun; what action did this malignant mouther of verses ever do for your good?   He can point to none.   There is not a single decree, small or great, with reference to the interests of the city, standing in the name of Aeschines.   If he asserts that there is, let him produce it in the time allotted to me.   But no such decree exists.   In that case, however, only two alternatives are possible: either he had no fault to find at the time with my policy, and therefore made no proposal contrary to it; or else he was seeking the advantage of the enemy, and therefore refrained from bringing forward any better policy than mine.

140   Did he then abstain from speaking, as he abstained from proposing any motion, when any mischief was to be done? On the contrary, no one else had a chance of speaking. But though, apparently, the city could endure everything else, and he could do everything else unobserved, there was one final deed which was the culmination of all that he had done before.   Upon this he expended all that multitude of words, as he went through the decrees relating to the Amphisseans, in the hope of distorting the truth.   But the

truth cannot be distorted. It is impossible. Never will
you wash away the stain of your actions there ! You will
not say enough for that !

I call upon all the gods and goddesses who protect this land 141
of Attica, in the presence of you all, men of Athens ; and
upon Apollo of Pytho, the paternal deity [n] of this city, and
I pray to them all, that if I should speak the truth to you—
if I spoke it at that very time without delay, in the presence
of the people, when first I saw this abominable man setting his
hand to this business (for I knew it, I knew it at once),—that
then they may give me good fortune and life : but if, to
gratify my hatred or any private quarrel, I am now bringing
a false accusation against this man, then they may take from
me the fruition of every blessing.

Why have I uttered this imprecation with such vehemence 142
and earnestness ? Because, although I have documents, lying
in the public archives, by which I will prove the facts clearly ;
although I know that you remember what was done ; I have
still the fear that he may be thought too insignificant a man
to have done all the evil which he has wrought—as indeed
happened before, when he caused the ruin of the unhappy
Phocians by the false report which he brought home. For the 143
war at Amphissa, which was the cause of Philip's coming
to Elateia, and of one being chosen [n] commander of the Amphictyons, who overthrew the fortunes of the Hellenes—*he*
it is who helped to get it up ; he, in his sole person, is to blame
for disasters to which no equal can be found. I protested at
the time, and cried out, before the Assembly, 'You are bringing war into Attica, Aeschines—an Amphictyonic War.' But
a packed group of his supporters refused to let me speak, while
the rest were amazed, and imagined that I was bringing

a baseless charge against him, out of personal animosity.

144 But what the true nature of these proceedings was, men of Athens—why this plan was contrived, and how it was executed—you must hear from me to-day, since you were prevented from doing so at the time. You will behold a business cunningly organized; you will advance greatly in your knowledge of public affairs; and you will see what cleverness there was in Philip.

145 Philip had no prospect of seeing the end of the war with you, or ridding himself of it, unless he could make the Thebans and Thessalians enemies of Athens. For although the war was being wretchedly and inefficiently conducted by your generals, he was nevertheless suffering infinite damage from the war itself and from the freebooters. The exportation of the produce of his country and the importation of what

146 he needed were both impossible. Moreover, he was not at that time superior to you at sea, nor could he reach Attica, if the Thessalians would not follow him, or the Thebans give him a passage through their country; and although he was overcoming in the field the generals whom you sent out, such as they were (for of this I say nothing), he found himself suffering from the geographical conditions themselves, and from the nature of the resources [n] which

147 either side possessed. Now if he tried to encourage either the Thessalians or the Thebans to march against you in order to further his own quarrel, no one, he thought, would pay any attention to him; but if he adopted their own common grounds of action and were chosen commander, he hoped to find it easier to deceive or to persuade them, as the case might be. What then does he do? He attempts (and observe with what skill) to stir up an Amphictyonic

War, and a disturbance in connexion with the meeting of
the Council. For he thought that they would at once find 148
that they needed his help, to deal with these. Now if one
of his own or his allies' representatives on the Council [n]
brought the matter forward, he thought that both the
Thebans and the Thessalians would regard the proceeding
with suspicion, and that all would be on their guard : but
if it was an Athenian, sent by you, his adversaries, that did
so, he would easily escape detection—as, in fact, happened.
How then did he manage this ? He hired Aeschines. No 149
one, I suppose, either realized beforehand what was going
on or guarded against it—that is how such affairs are usually
conducted here ; Aeschines was nominated a delegate to the
Council; three or four people held up their hands for him, and
he was declared elected. But when, bearing with him the
prestige of this city, he reached the Amphictyons, he dismissed
and closed his eyes to all other considerations, and proceeded
to perform the task for which he had been hired. He composed
and recited a story, in attractive language, of the way in which
the Cirrhaean territory had come to be dedicated ; and with 150
this he persuaded the members of the Council, who were
unused to rhetoric and did not foresee what was about to
happen, that they should resolve to make the circuit of the
territory,[n] which the Amphisseans said they were cultivating
because it was their own, while he alleged that it was part
of the consecrated land. The Locrians were not bringing
any suit against us, or taking any such action as (in order to
justify himself) he now falsely alleges. You may know this from
the following consideration. It was clearly impossible [n] for the
Locrians to bring a suit against Athens to an actual issue, without summoning us. Who then served the summons upon us ?

G

Before what authority was it served ? Tell us who knows :
point to him. You cannot do so. It was a hollow and a false
151 pretext of which you thus made a wrongful use. While the
Amphictyons were making the circuit of the territory in
accordance with Aeschines' suggestion, the Locrians fell
upon them and came near to shooting them all down with
their spears ; some of the members of the Council they even
carried off with them. And now that complaints and hostilities had been stirred up against the Amphisseans, in consequence of these proceedings, the command was first held
by Cottyphus, and his force was drawn from the Amphictyonic Powers alone. But since some did not come, and those
who came did nothing, the men who had been suborned for
the purpose—villains of long standing, chosen from the Thessalians and from the traitors in other States—took steps with a
view to entrusting the affair to Philip, as commander, at the
152 next meeting of the Council. They had adopted arguments
of a persuasive kind. Either, they said, the Amphictyons
must themselves contribute funds, maintain mercenaries, and
fine those who refused to do so ; or they must elect Philip.
To make a long story short, the result was that Philip was
appointed. And immediately afterwards, having collected
a force and crossed the Pass, ostensibly on his way to the
territory of Cirrha, he bids a long farewell to the Cirrhaeans
153 and Locrians, and seizes Elateia. Now if the Thebans had not
changed their policy at once, upon seeing this, and joined us,
the trouble would have descended upon the city in full force,
like a torrent in winter. As it was, the Thebans checked him
for the moment ; chiefly, men of Athens, through the goodwill of some Heavenly Power towards us ; but secondarily,
so far as it lay in one man's power, through me also. (*To the*

clerk.)   Now give me the decrees in question, and the dates of each proceeding ; (*to the jury*) that you may know what trouble this abominable creature stirred up, unpunished. (*To the clerk.*)   Read me the decrees.   154

[*The decrees of the Amphictyons are read.*]

(*To the clerk.*)   Now read the dates of these proceedings. 155
(*To the jury.*)   They are the dates at which Aeschines was delegate to the Council.   (*To the clerk.*)   Read.

[*The dates are read.*]

Now give me the letter which Philip sent to his allies 156
in the Peloponnese, when the Thebans failed to obey his summons.   For from this, too, you may clearly see that he concealed the real reason for his action—the fact that he was taking measures against Hellas and the Thebans and yourselves—and pretended to represent the common cause and the will of the Amphictyons. And the man who provided him with all these occasions and pretexts was Aeschines.   (*To the clerk.*)   Read.

[*Philip's letter is read.*]   157

You see that he avoids the mention of his own reasons for 158
action, and takes refuge in those provided by the Amphictyons.   Who was it that helped him to prepare such a case ? Who put such pretexts at his disposal ?   Who is most to blame for the disasters that have taken place ?   Is it not Aeschines ? And so, men of Athens, you must not go about saying that Hellas has suffered such things as these at the hands of one man.[n]   I call Earth and Heaven to witness, that it was at the hands, not of one man, but of many villains in each State. And of these Aeschines is one ; and, had I to speak the truth 159
without any reserve, I should not hesitate to describe him

as the incarnate curse of all alike—men, regions or cities—
that have been ruined since then. For he who supplied
the seed is responsible for the crop. I wonder that you
did not turn away your eyes at the very sight of him :
but a cloud of darkness seems to hang between you and
the truth.

160   I find that in dealing with the measures taken by Aeschines
for the injury of his country, I have reached the time when
I must speak of my own statesmanship in opposition to these
measures ; and it is fair that you should listen to this, for
many reasons, but above all because it will be a shameful
thing, if, when I have faced the actual realities of hard work
for you, you will not even suffer the story of them to be told.

161 For when I saw the Thebans, and (I may almost say) yourselves as well, being led by the corrupt partisans of Philip
in either State to overlook, without taking a single precaution
against it, the thing which was really dangerous to both peoples
and needed their utmost watchfulness—the unhindered growth
of Philip's power ; while, on the contrary, you were quite
ready to entertain ill-feeling and to quarrel with one another ;
I kept unceasing watch to prevent this. Nor did I rely only
on my own judgement in thinking that this was what your

162 interest required. I knew that Aristophon, and afterwards
Eubulus, always wished to bring about this friendly union,
and that, often as they opposed one another in other matters,
they always agreed in this. Cunning fox ! While they lived,
you hung about them and flattered them ; yet now that they
are dead, you do not see that you are attacking them. For
your censure of my policy in regard to Thebes is far more
a denunciation of them than of me, since they were before me

163 in approving of that alliance. But I return to my previous

point—that it was when Aeschines had brought about the war at Amphissa, and the others, his accomplices, had effectually helped him to create the ill-feeling against the Thebans, that Philip marched against us. For it was to render this possible that their attempt to throw the two cities into collision was made ; and had we not roused ourselves a little before it was too late, we should never have been able to regain the lost ground ; to such a length had these men carried matters. What the relations between the two peoples already were, you will know when you have heard these decrees and replies. (*To the clerk.*) Take these and read them.

[*The decrees are read.*]   164, 165

(*To the clerk.*) Now read the replies.   166

[*The replies are read.*]   167

Having established such relations between the cities, 168 through the agency of these men, and being elated by these decrees and replies, Philip came with his army and seized Elateia, thinking that under no circumstances whatever should we and the Thebans join in unison after this. And though the commotion which followed in the city is known to you all, let me relate to you briefly just the bare facts.

It was evening, and one had come to the Prytanes [n] with 169 the news that Elateia had been taken. Upon this they rose up from supper without delay ; some of them drove the occupants out of the booths in the market-place and set fire to the wicker-work ; [n] others sent for the generals and summoned the trumpeter ; and the city was full of commotion. On the morrow, at break of day, the Prytanes summoned the Council to the Council-Chamber, while you

made your way to the Assembly ; and before the Council
had transacted its business and passed its draft-resolution,[n]
170 the whole people was seated on the hill-side.[n] And now,
when the Council had arrived, and the Prytanes had reported
the intelligence which they had received, and had brought
forward the messenger, and he had made his statement, the
herald proceeded to ask, 'Who wishes to speak?' But no one
came forward ; and though the herald repeated the question
many times, still no one rose, though all the generals were
present, and all the orators, and the voice of their country
was calling for some one to speak for her deliverance. For
the voice of the herald, uttered in accordance with the laws,
is rightly to be regarded as the common voice of our country.
171 And yet, if it was for those to come forward who wished
for the deliverance of the city, all of you and all the other
Athenians would have risen, and proceeded to the platform,
for I am certain that you all wished for her deliverance.
If it was for the wealthiest, the Three Hundred [n] would
have risen ; and if it was for those who had both these qualifi-
cations—loyalty to the city and wealth—then those would
have risen, who subsequently made those large donations ;
172 for it was loyalty and wealth that led them so to do. But
that crisis and that day called, it seems, not merely for a man
of loyalty and wealth, but for one who had also followed
the course of events closely from the first, and had come
to a true conclusion as to the motive and the aim with which
Philip was acting as he was. For no one who was unacquainted
with these, and had not scrutinized them from an early
period, was any the more likely, for all his loyalty and wealth,
to know what should be done, or to be able to advise you.
173 The man who was needed was found that day in me. I came

forward and addressed you in words which I ask you to listen to with attention, for two reasons—first, because I would have you realize that I was the only orator or politician who did not desert his post as a loyal citizen in the hour of danger, but was found there, speaking and proposing what your need required, in the midst of the terror; and secondly, because by the expenditure of a small amount of time, you will be far better qualified for the future in the whole art of political administration. My words then were these: 174 ' Those who are unduly disturbed by the idea that Philip can count upon the support of Thebes do not, I think, understand the present situation. For I am quite sure that, if this were so, we should have heard of his being, not at Elateia, but on our own borders. At the same time, I understand quite well, that he has come to prepare the way for himself at Thebes. Listen,' I said, ' while I tell you the 175 true state of affairs. Philip already has at his disposal all the Thebans whom he could win over either by bribery or by deception; and those who have resisted him from the first and are opposing him now, he has no chance of winning. What then is his design and object in seizing Elateia? He wishes, by making a display of force in their neighbourhood and bringing up his army, to encourage and embolden his own friends, and to strike terror into his enemies, that so they may either concede out of terror what they now refuse, or may be compelled. Now,' I said, ' if we make 176 up our minds at the present moment to remember any ill-natured action which the Thebans may have done us, and to distrust them on the assumption that they are on the side of our enemies, we shall be doing, in the first place, just what Philip would pray for: and further, I am afraid that his present opponents may then welcome him, that all may philippize [n] with one consent, and that he and they may march to Attica together. If, however, you follow my advice, and give your minds to the problem before us, instead of to contentious criticism of anything that I may say, I believe that I shall be able to win your approval for my proposals, and to dispel the danger which threatens the city.

177 What then must you do? You must first moderate your present alarm, and then change your attitude, and be alarmed, all of you, for the Thebans. They are far more within the reach of disaster than we: it is they whom the danger threatens first. Secondly, those who are of military age, with the cavalry, must march to Eleusis,[n] and let every one see that you yourselves are in arms; in order that those who sympathize with you in Thebes may be enabled to speak in defence of the right, with the same freedom that their opponents enjoy, when they see that, just as those who are trying to sell their country to Philip have a force ready to help them at Elateia, so those who would struggle for freedom have you ready at hand to help them, and to go

178 to their aid, if any one attacks them. Next I bid you elect ten envoys, and give them full authority, with the generals, to decide the time of their own journey to Thebes, and to order the march of the troops. But when the envoys arrive in Thebes, how do I advise that they should handle the matter? I ask your special attention to this. They must require nothing of the Thebans—to do so at such a moment would be shameful; but they must undertake that we will go to their aid, if they bid us do so, on the ground that they are in extreme peril, and that we foresee the future better than they; in order that, if they accept our offer and take our

advice, we may have secured our object, and our action may wear an aspect worthy of this city; or, if after all we are unsuccessful, the Thebans may have themselves to blame for any mistakes which they now make, while we shall have done nothing disgraceful or ignoble.' When I had spoken 179 these words, and others in the same strain, I left the platform. All joined in commending these proposals; no one said a word in opposition; and I did not speak thus, and then fail to move a motion; nor move a motion, and then fail to serve as envoy; nor serve as envoy, and then fail to persuade the Thebans. I carried the matter through in person from beginning to end, and gave myself up unreservedly to meet the dangers which encompassed the city. (*To the clerk.*) Bring me the resolution which was then passed.

But now, Aeschines, how would you have me describe 180 your part, and how mine, that day? Shall I call myself, as you would call me by way of abuse and disparagement, *Battalus*? [n] and you, no ordinary hero even, but a real stage-hero, *Cresphontes* or *Creon*,[n] or—the character which you cruelly murdered at Collytus [n]—*Oenomaus*? Then I, Battalus of Paeania, proved myself of more value to my country in that crisis than Oenomaus of Cothocidae. In fact you were of no service on any occasion, while I played the part which became a good citizen throughout. (*To the clerk.*) Read this decree.

[*The decree of Demosthenes is read.*]   181–7

This was the first step towards our new relations with 188 Thebes, and the beginning of a settlement. Up to this time the cities had been inveigled into mutual hostility, hatred, and mistrust by these men. But this decree caused the peril that encompassed the city to pass away like a cloud. It was for an honest citizen, if he had any better plan than mine, to make it public at the time, instead of attacking me now.

189 The true counsellor and the dishonest accuser, unlike as they are in everything, differ most of all in this : the one declares his opinion before the event, and freely surrenders himself as responsible, to those who follow his advice, to Fortune, to circumstances, to any one.[n] The other is silent when he ought to speak, and then carps at anything

190 untoward that may happen. That crisis, as I have said, was the opportunity for a man who cared for his country, the opportunity for honest speaking. But so much further than I need will I go, that if any one can *now* point to any better course—or any course at all except that which I chose —I admit my guilt. If any one has discovered any course to-day, which would have been for our advantage, had we followed it at the time, I admit that it ought not to have escaped me. But if there neither is nor was such a possibility; if even now, even to-day, no one can mention any such course, what was the counsellor of the people to do ? Had he not to choose the best of the plans which suggested themselves

191 and were feasible ? This I did. For the herald asked the question, Aeschines, 'Who wishes to speak?' not 'Who wishes to bring accusations about the past?' nor 'Who wishes to guarantee the future?' And while you sat speechless in the Assembly throughout that period, I came forward and spoke. Since, however, you did not do so then, at least inform us now, and tell us what words, which should have been upon my lips, were left unspoken, what precious opportunity, offered to the city, was left unused, by me ? What alliance was there, what course of action,

to which I ought, by preference, to have guided my countrymen ?

But with all mankind the past is always dismissed from 192 consideration, and no one under any circumstances proposes to deliberate about it. It is the future or the present that make their call upon a statesman's duty. Now at that time the danger was partly in the future, and partly already present ; and instead of cavilling disingenuously at the results, consider the principle of my policy under such circumstances. For in everything the final issue falls out as Heaven wills ; but the principle which he follows itself reveals the mind of the statesman. Do not, therefore, count it a crime on my 193 part, that Philip proved victorious in the battle. The issue of that event lay with God, not with me. But show me that I did not adopt every expedient that was possible, so far as human reason could calculate ; that I did not carry out my plan honestly and diligently, with exertions greater than my strength could bear ; or that the policy which I initiated was not honourable, and worthy of Athens, and indeed necessary : and then denounce me, but not before. But if the thunderbolt 194 [or the storm] which fell has proved too mighty, not only for us, but for all the other Hellenes, what are we to do ? It is as though a ship-owner, who had done all that he could to ensure safety, and had equipped the ship with all that he thought would enable her to escape destruction, and had then met with a tempest in which the tackling had been strained or even broken to pieces, were to be held responsible for the wreck of the vessel. 'Why,' he would say, 'I was not steering the ship '—just as I was not the general [n]— 'I had no power over Fortune : she had power over everything.' But consider and observe this point. If it was fated 195 that we should fare as we did, even when we had the Thebans to help us in the struggle, what must we have expected, if we had not had even them for our allies, but they had joined Philip ?—and this was the object for which Philip employed [n] every tone that he could command. And if, when the battle took place, as it did, three days' march from Attica, the city was encompassed by such peril and terror, what should we have had to expect, if this same disaster had occurred anywhere within the borders of our own country ? Do you realize that, as it was, a single day, and a second, and a third gave us the power to rally, to collect our forces, to take breath, to do much that made for the deliverance of the city : but that had it been otherwise—it is not well, however, to speak of things which we have not had to experience, thanks to the goodwill of one of the gods, and to the protection which the city obtained for herself in this alliance, which you denounce.

196   The whole of this long argument, gentlemen of the jury, is addressed to yourselves and to the circle of listeners outside the bar ; for to this despicable man it would have been enough to address a short, plain sentence. If to you alone, Aeschines, the future was clear, before it came, you should have given warning, when the city was deliberating upon the subject ; but if you had no such foreknowledge, you have the same ignorance to answer for as others. Why then should you make these charges against me, any more than I against you ?

197 For I have been a better citizen than you with regard to this very matter of which I am speaking—I am not as yet talking of anything else—just in so far as I gave myself up to the policy which all thought expedient, neither shrinking from nor regarding any personal risk ; while you

neither offered any better proposals than mine (for then they would not have followed mine), nor yet made yourself useful in advancing mine in any way. What the most worthless of men, the bitterest enemy of the city, would do, you are found to have done, when all was over ; and at the same time as the irreconcilable enemies of the city, Aristratus in Naxos, and Aristoleos in Thasos, are bringing the friends of Athens to trial, Aeschines, in Athens itself, is accusing Demosthenes. But surely one who treasured up [n] the misfortunes 198 of the Hellenes, that he might win glory from them for himself, deserved to perish rather than to stand as the accuser of another ; and one who has profited by the very same crisis as the enemies of the city cannot possibly be loyal to his country. You prove it, moreover, by the life you live, the actions you do, the measures you take—and the measures, too, that you do not take. Is anything being done which seems advantageous to the city ? Aeschines is speechless. Has any obstruction, any untoward event occurred ? There you find Aeschines, like a rupture or a sprain, which wakes into life, so soon as any trouble overtakes the body.

But since he bears so hardly upon the results, I desire to 199 say what may even be a paradox ; and let no one, in the name of Heaven, be amazed at the length to which I go, but give a kindly consideration to what I say. Even if what was to come was plain to all beforehand ; even if all foreknew it ; even if you, Aeschines, had been crying with a loud voice in warning and protestation—you who uttered not so much as a sound ; even then, I say, it was not right for the city to abandon her course, if she had any regard for her fame, or for our forefathers, or for the ages to come. As it is, she is 200 thought, no doubt, to have failed to secure her object—

as happens to all alike, whenever God wills it : but then, by
abandoning in favour of Philip her claim to take the lead of
others, she must have incurred the blame of having betrayed
them all. Had she surrendered without a struggle those
claims in defence of which our forefathers faced every
imaginable peril, who would not have cast scorn upon you,
Aeschines—upon you, I say ; not, I trust, upon Athens nor
201 upon me ? In God's name, with what faces should we have
looked upon those who came to visit the city, if events had
come round to the same conclusion as they now have—if
Philip had been chosen as commander and lord of all, and we
had stood apart, while others carried on the struggle to
prevent these things ; and that, although the city had never
yet in time past preferred an inglorious security to the
202 hazardous vindication of a noble cause ? What Hellene,
what foreigner, does not know, that the Thebans, and the
Spartans, who were powerful still earlier, and the Persian
king would all gratefully and gladly have allowed Athens
to take what she liked and keep all that was her own, if she
would do the bidding of another, and let another take
203 the first place in Hellas ? But this was not, it appears, the
tradition of the Athenians ; it was not tolerable ; it was
not in their nature. From the beginning of time no one
had ever yet succeeded in persuading the city to throw in
her lot with those who were strong, but unrighteous in their
dealings, and to enjoy the security of servitude. Throughout
all time she has maintained her perilous struggle for pre-
204 eminence, honour, and glory. And this policy you look upon
as so lofty, so proper to your own national character, that, of
your forefathers also, it is those who have acted thus that
you praise most highly. And naturally. For who would not

admire the courage of those men, who did not fear to leave their land [n] and their city, and to embark upon their ships, that they might not do the bidding of another ; who chose for their general Themistocles (who had counselled them thus), and stoned Cyrsilus to death, when he gave his voice for submission to a master's orders—and not him alone, for your wives stoned his wife also to death. For the Athenians 205 of that day did not look for an orator or a general who would enable them to live in happy servitude ; they cared not to live at all, unless they might live in freedom. For every one of them felt that he had come into being, not for his father and his mother alone, but also for his country. And wherein lies the difference ? He who thinks he was born for his parents alone awaits the death which destiny assigns him in the course of nature : but he who thinks he was born for his country also will be willing to die, that he may not see her in bondage, and will look upon the outrages and the indignities that he must needs bear in a city that is in bondage as more to be dreaded than death.

Now were I attempting to argue that *I* had induced you 206 to show a spirit worthy of your forefathers, there is not a man who might not rebuke me with good reason. But in fact, I am declaring that such principles as these are your own ; I am showing that *before* my time the city displayed this spirit, though I claim that I, too, have had some share, as your servant, in carrying out your policy in detail. But in 207 denouncing the policy as a whole, in bidding you be harsh with me, as one who has brought terrors and dangers upon the city, the prosecutor, in his eagerness to deprive me of my distinction at the present moment, is trying to rob you of praises that will last throughout all time. For if you condemn the defendant on the ground that my policy was not for the best, men will think that your own judgement has been wrong, and that it was not through the unkindness of fortune 208 that you suffered what befell you. But it cannot,[n] it cannot be that you were wrong, men of Athens, when you took upon you the struggle for freedom and deliverance. No! by those who at Marathon bore the brunt of the peril—our forefathers. No! by those who at Plataeae drew up their battle-line, by those who at Salamis, by those who off Artemisium fought the fight at sea, by the many who lie in the sepulchres where the People laid them, brave men, all alike deemed worthy by their country, Aeschines, of the same honour and the same obsequies—not the successful or the victorious alone! And she acted justly. For all these have done that which it was the duty of brave men to do; but their fortune has 209 been that which Heaven assigned to each. Accursed, poring pedant![n] if you, in your anxiety to deprive me of the honour and the kindness shown to me by my countrymen, re-counted trophies and battles and deeds of long ago—and of which of them did this present trial demand the mention?— what spirit was I to take upon me, when I mounted the plat-form, I who came forward to advise the city how she should maintain her pre-eminence? Tell me, third-rate actor! The spirit of one who would propose things unworthy of 210 this people? I should indeed have deserved to die! For you too, men of Athens, ought not to judge private suits and public in the same spirit. The business transactions of every-day life must be viewed in the light of the special law and practice associated with each; but the public policy of statesmen must be judged by the principles that your fore-fathers set before them. And if you believe that you should

act worthily of them, then, whenever you come into court
to try a public suit, each of you must imagine that with his
staff [n] and his ticket there is entrusted to him also the spirit
of his country.

But I have entered upon the subject of your forefathers' 211
achievements, and have passed over certain decrees and transactions. I desire, therefore, to return to the point from
which I digressed.

When we came to Thebes, we found envoys there from
Philip, and from the Thessalians and his other allies—our
friends in terror, his full of confidence. And to show you
that I am not saying this now to suit my own purpose, read
the letter which we, your envoys, dispatched without delay.
The prosecutor, however, has exercised the art of misrepresen- 212
tation to so extravagant a degree, that he attributes to
circumstances, not to me, any satisfactory result that was
achieved ; but for everything that fell out otherwise, he lays
the blame upon me and the fortune that attends me. In his
eyes, apparently, I, the counsellor and orator, have no share
in the credit for what was accomplished as the result of
oratory and debate ; while I must bear the blame alone
for the misfortunes which we suffered in arms, and as a
result of generalship. What more brutal, more damnable
misrepresentation can be conceived ? (*To the clerk.*) Read
the letter.

[The letter is read.]

When they had convened the Assembly, they gave audience 213
to the other side first, on the ground that they occupied
the position of allies ; and these came forward and delivered
harangues full of the praises of Philip and of accusations against
yourselves, recalling everything that you had ever done

in opposition to the Thebans. The sum of it all was that they
required the Thebans to show their gratitude for the benefits
which they had received from Philip, and to exact the penalty
for the injuries they had received from you, in whichever
way they preferred—either by letting them march through
their country against you, or by joining them in the invasion
of Attica ; and they showed (as they thought) that the result
of the course which they advised would be that the herds
and slaves and other valuables of Attica would find their
way into Boeotia ; while the result of what (as they alleged)
you were about to propose would be that those of Boeotia
214 would be plundered in consequence of the war. They said
much more, but all tending to the same effect. As for our
reply, I would give my whole life to tell it you in detail ;
but I fear lest, now that those times have gone by, you may
feel as if a very deluge [n] had overwhelmed all, and may regard
anything that is said on the subject as vanity and vexation.
But hear at least what we persuaded them to do, and their
answer to us. (*To the clerk.*) Take this and read it.

[*The answer of the Thebans is read.*]

215   After this they invited and summoned you ; you marched ;
you went to their aid ; and (to pass over the events which
intervened) they received you in so friendly a spirit that while
their infantry and cavalry were encamped outside the walls,[n]
they welcomed your troops into their houses, within the city,
among their children and wives, and all that was most
precious to them. Three eulogies did the Thebans pronounce
upon you before the world that day, and those of the most
honourable kind—the first upon your courage, the second
upon your righteousness, the third upon your self-control.

For when they chose to side with you in the struggle, rather than against you, they judged that your courage was greater, and your requests more righteous, than Philip's ; and when they placed in your power what they and all men guard most jealously, their children and wives, they showed their confidence in your self-control. In all these points, men of Athens, 216 your conduct proved that their judgement had been correct. For the force came into the city; but no one made a single complaint—not even an unfounded complaint—against you ; so virtuously did you conduct yourselves. And twice you fought by their side, in the earliest battles—the battle by the river [n] and the winter-battle [n]—and showed yourselves, not only irreproachable, but even admirable, in your discipline, your equipment, and your enthusiasm. These things called forth expressions of thanks to you from other states, and sacrifices and processions to the gods from yourselves. And I should 217 like to ask Aeschines whether, when all this was happening, and the city was full of pride and joy and thanksgiving, he joined in the sacrifices and the rejoicing of the multitude, or whether he sat at home grieving and groaning and angry at the good fortune of his country. If he was present, and was seen in his place with the rest, surely his present action is atrocious—nay, even impious—when he asks you, who have taken an oath by the gods, to vote to-day that those very things were not excellent, of whose excellence he himself on that day made the gods his witnesses. If he was not present, then surely he deserves to die many times, for grieving at the sight of the things which brought rejoicing to others. (*To the clerk.*) Now read these decrees also.

[The decrees ordering sacrifices are read.]

218 Thus we were occupied at that time with sacrifices, while
the Thebans were reflecting how they had been saved by
our help ; and those who, in consequence of my opponents'
proceedings, had expected that they would themselves stand
in need of help, found themselves, after all, helping others,
in consequence of the action they took upon my advice.
But what the tone of Philip's utterance was, and how greatly
he was confounded by what had happened, you can learn from
his letter, which he sent to the Peloponnese. (*To the clerk.*)
Take these and read them : (*to the jury*) that you may
know what was effected by my perseverance, by my travels,
by the hardships I endured, by all those decrees of which
Aeschines spoke so disparagingly just now.

219 You have had, as you know, many great and famous
orators, men of Athens, before my time—Callistratus
himself, Aristophon, Cephalus, Thrasybulus, and a vast
number of others. Yet not one of these ever gave himself
up entirely to the State for any purpose: the mover of a decree
would not serve as ambassador, the ambassador would not
move the decree. Each left himself, at one and the same time,
some respite from work, and somewhere to lay the blame,[n]
220 in case of accidents. 'Well,' some one may say, 'did *you*
so excel them in force and boldness, as to do everything
yourself ? ' I do not say that. But so strong was my con-
viction of the seriousness of the danger that had overtaken
the city, that I felt that I ought not to give my personal
safety any place whatever in my thoughts ; it was
enough for a man to do his duty and to leave nothing
221 undone. And I was convinced with regard to myself—

foolishly perhaps, but still convinced—that no mover would make a better proposal, no agent would execute it better, no ambassador would be more eager or more honest in his mission, than I. For these reasons, I assigned every one of these offices to myself. (*To the clerk.*) Read Philip's letters.

[*Philip's letters are read.*]

To this condition, Aeschines, was Philip reduced by my 222 statesmanship. This was the tone of his utterances, though before this he used to threaten the city with many a bold word. For this I was deservedly crowned by those here assembled, and though you were present, you offered no opposition ; while Diondas, who indicted the proposer, did not obtain the necessary fraction of the votes. (*To the clerk.*) Read me these decrees, (*to the jury*) which escaped condemnation, and which Aeschines did not even indict.

[*The decrees are read.*]

These decrees, men of Athens, contain the very same 223 syllables, the very same words, as those which Aristonicus previously employed in his proposal, and which Ctesiphon, the defendant, has employed now ; and Aeschines neither prosecuted the proposer of them himself, nor supported the person who indicted him. Yet surely, if the charges which he is bringing against me to-day are true, he would have had better reason then for prosecuting Demomeles (the proposer of the decree) and Hypereides, than he has for prosecuting Ctesiphon. And why ? Because Ctesiphon can refer you to them—to 224 the decision of the courts, to the fact that Aeschines himself did not accuse them, though they had moved exactly what he has moved now, to the prohibition by law of further

prosecution in such cases, and to many other facts : whereas
then the case would have been tried on its merits, before
the defendant had got the advantage of any such precedent.
225 But of course it was impossible then for Aeschines to act
as he has acted now—to select out of many periods of
time long past, and many decrees, matters which no one
either knew or thought would be mentioned to-day ;
to misrepresent them, to change the dates, to put false
reasons for the actions taken in place of the true, and so
226 appear to have a case. At the time this was impossible.
Every word spoken then must have been spoken with the truth
in view, at no distance of time from the events, while you
still remembered all the facts and had them practically at
your fingers' ends. For that reason he evaded all investigation at the time ; and he has come before you now, in the
belief (I fancy) that you will make this a contest of oratory,
instead of an inquiry into our political careers, and that it
is upon our eloquence, not upon the interests of the city,
that you will decide.

227   Yes, and he ingeniously suggests that you ought to disregard
the opinion which you had of each of us when you left your
homes and came into court ; and that just as, when you draw
up an account in the belief that some one has a balance, you
nevertheless give way when you find that the counters all disappear[n] and leave nothing over, so now you should give your
adhesion to the conclusion which emerges from the argument.
Now observe how inherently rotten everything that springs
228 from dishonesty seems to be. By his very use of this ingenious
illustration he has confessed that to-day, at all events, our
respective characters are well established—that I am known
to speak for my country's good, and he to speak for Philip.

For unless that were your present conception of each of us, he would not have sought to change your view. And further, 229 I shall easily show you that it is not fair of him to ask you to alter this opinion—not by the use of counters—that is not how a political reckoning is made—but by briefly recalling each point to you, and treating you who hear me both as auditors of my account and witnesses to the facts. For that policy of mine which he denounces caused the Thebans, instead of joining Philip, as all expected them to do, in the invasion of our country, to range themselves by our side and stay his progress. It caused the war to take place not in Attica, but 230 on the confines of Boeotia, eighty miles from the city. Instead of our being harried and plundered by freebooters from Euboea, it gave peace to Attica from the side of the sea throughout the war. Instead of Philip's taking Byzantium and becoming master of the Hellespont, it caused the Byzantines to join us in the war against him. Can such achieve- 231 ments, think you, be reckoned up like counters? Are we to cancel them out,[n] rather than provide that they shall be remembered for all time? I need not now add that it fell to others to taste the barbarity which is to be seen in every case in which Philip got any one finally into his power; while you reaped (and quite rightly) the fruits of the generosity which he feigned while he was bringing within his grasp all that remained. But I pass this over.

Nay, I will not even hesitate to say, that one who wished 232 to review an orator's career straightforwardly and without misrepresentation, would not have included in his charges such matters as you just now spoke of—making up illustrations, and mimicking words and gestures. Of course the fortune which befell the Hellenes—surely you see this?—

was entirely due to my using this word instead of that, or waving my hand in one direction rather than the other!

233 He would have inquired, by reference to the actual facts, what resources and what forces the city had at her command when I entered political life; what I subsequently collected for her when I took control; and what was the condition of our adversaries. Then if I had diminished our forces, he would have proved that the fault lay at my door; but if I had greatly increased them, he would have abstained from deliberate misrepresentation. But since you have avoided such an inquiry, I will undertake it; and do you, gentlemen, observe whether my argument is just.

234   The military resources of the city included the islanders—and not all, but only the weakest. For neither Chios nor Rhodes nor Corcyra was with us. Their contribution in money came to 45 talents, and these had been collected in advance.[n] Infantry and cavalry, besides our own, we had none. But the circumstance which was most alarming to us and most favourable to our enemies was that these men had contrived that all our neighbours should be more inclined to enmity than to friendship—the Megareans, the Thebans,

235 and the Euboeans. Such was the position of the city at the time; and what I say admits of no contradiction. Now consider the position of Philip, with whom our conflict lay. In the first place, he held absolute sway over his followers—and this for purposes of war is the greatest of all advantages. Next, his followers had their weapons in their hands always. Then he was well off for money, and did whatever he resolved to do, without giving warning of it by decrees, or debating about it in public, or being put on trial by dishonest accusers, or defending himself against indictments for illegality, or

being bound to render an account to any one. He was himself absolute master, commander, and lord of all. But 236 I who was set to oppose him—for this inquiry too it is just to make—what had I under my control? Nothing! For, to begin with, the very right to address you— the only right I had—you extended to Philip's hirelings in the same measure as to me; and as often as they defeated me—and this frequently happened, whatever the reason on each occasion—so often you went away leaving a resolution recorded in favour of the enemy. But in spite of 237 all these disadvantages, I won for you the alliance of the Euboeans, Achaeans, Corinthians, Thebans, Megareans, Leucadians, and Corcyreans, from whom were collected— apart from their citizen-troops—15,000 mercenaries and 2,000 cavalry. And I instituted a money-contribution, on as 238 large a scale as I could. But if you refer,[n] Aeschines, to what was fair as between ourselves and the Thebans or the Byzantines or the Euboeans—if at this time you talk to us of equal shares—you must be ignorant, in the first place, of the fact that in former days also, out of those ships of war, three hundred [n] in all, which fought for the Hellenes, Athens provided two hundred, and did not think herself unfairly used, or let herself be seen arraigning those who had counselled her action, or taking offence at the arrangement. It would have been shameful. No! men saw her rendering thanks to Heaven, because when a common peril beset the Hellenes, she had provided double as much as all the rest to secure the deliverance of all. Moreover, it is but a hollow benefit that you 239 are conferring upon your countrymen by your dishonest charges against me. Why do you tell them *now*, what course they ought to have taken? Why did you not propose such a course at the time (for you were in Athens, and were present) if it was possible in the midst of those critical times, when we had to accept, not what we chose, but what circumstances allowed ; since there was one at hand, bidding against us, and ready to welcome those whom we rejected, and to pay them into the bargain.

240 But if I am accused to-day, for what I have actually done, what if at the time I had haggled over these details, and the other states had gone off and joined Philip, and he had become master at once of Euboea and Thebes and Byzantium ? What do you think these impious men would then

241 have done ? What would they have said ? Would they not have declared that the states had been surrendered ? that they had been driven away, when they wished to be on your side ? ' See,' they would have said (would they not ?), ' he has obtained through the Byzantines the command of the Hellespont and the control of the corn trade of Hellas ; and through the Thebans a trying border war has been brought into Attica ; and owing to the pirates who sail from Euboea, the sea has become unnavigable,' and much

242 more in addition. A villainous thing, men of Athens, is the dishonest accuser always—villainous, and in every way malignant and fault-finding! Aye, and this miserable creature is a fox by nature, that has never done anything honest or gentlemanly—a very tragical ape, a clodhopping Oeno-

243 maus, a counterfeit orator! Where is the profit to your country from your cleverness ? Do you instruct us now about things that are past ? It is as though a doctor, when he was paying his visits to the sick, were to give them no advice or instructions to enable them to become free from their illness, but, when one of his patients died and the customary offerings [n]

were being paid him, were to explain, as he followed to the tomb, ' if this man had done such and such things, he would not have died.' Crazy fool! Do you tell us this *now* ?

Nor again will you find that the defeat—if you exult at it, **244** when you ought to groan, accursed man !—was determined by anything that was within my control. Consider the question thus. In no place to which I was sent by you as ambassador, did I ever come away defeated by the ambassadors of Philip—not from Thessaly nor from Ambracia, not from the Illyrians nor from the Thracian princes, not from Byzantium nor from any other place, nor yet, on the last occasion, from Thebes. But every place in which his ambassadors were defeated in argument, he proceeded to attack and subdue by force of arms. Do you then require **245** those places at *my* hands ? Are you not ashamed to jeer at a man as a coward, and in the same breath to require him to prove superior, by his own unaided efforts, to the army of Philip—and that with no weapons to use but words ? For what else was at my disposal ? I could not control the spirit of each soldier, or the fortune of the combatants, or the generalship displayed, of which, in your perversity, you demand an account from me. No ; but every investi- **246** gation that can be made as regards those duties for which an orator should be held responsible, I bid you make. I crave no mercy. And what are those duties ? To discern events in their beginnings, to foresee what is coming, and to fore-warn others. These things I have done. Again, it is his duty to reduce to the smallest possible compass, wherever he finds them, the slowness, the hesitation, the ignorance, the contentiousness, which are the errors inseparably connected

with the constitution of all city-states ; while, on the other
hand, he must stimulate men to unity, friendship, and eagerness to perform their duty. All these things I have done,
and no one can discover any dereliction of duty on my part

247 at any time. If one were to ask any person whatever, by what
means Philip had accomplished the majority of his successes,
every one would reply that it was by means of his army,
and by giving presents and corrupting those in charge of
affairs. Now I had no control or command of the forces :
neither, then, does the responsibility for anything that was
done in that sphere concern me. And further, in the matter
of being or not being corrupted by bribes, I have defeated
Philip. For just as the bidder has conquered one who accepts
his money, if he effects his purchase, so one who refuses to
accept it [and is not corrupted] has conquered the bidder.
In all, therefore, in which I am concerned, the city has suffered
no defeat.

248   The justification, then, with which I furnished the defendant for such a motion as he proposed with regard to me,
consisted (along with many other points) of the facts which
I have described, and others like them. I will now proceed
to that justification which all of you supplied. For immediately after the battle, the People, who knew and had seen
all that I did, and now stood in the very midst of the peril
and terror, at a moment when it would not have been sur-
prising if the majority had shown some harshness towards
me—the People, I say, in the first place carried my proposals
for ensuring the safety of the city ; and all the measures
undertaken for its protection—the disposition of the garrisons,
the entrenchments, the funds for the fortifications—were
all provided for by decrees which I proposed. And, in the

second place, when the People chose a corn-commissioner, out of all Athens they elected me. Subsequently all those 249 who were interested in injuring me combined, and assailed me with indictments, prosecutions after audit, impeachments, and all such proceedings—not in their own names at first, but through the agency of men behind whom, they thought, they would best be screened against recognition. For you doubtless know and remember that during the early part of that period I was brought to trial every day ; and neither the desperation of Sosicles, nor the dishonest misrepresentations of Philocrates,[n] nor the frenzy of Diondas and Melantus, nor any other expedient, was left untried by them against me. And in all these trials, thanks to the gods above all, but secondarily to you and the rest of the Athenians, I was acquitted—and justly ; for such a decision is in accordance both with truth and with the credit of jurors who have taken their oath, and given a verdict in conformity with it. So 250 whenever I was impeached, and you absolved me and did not give the prosecutor the necessary fraction of the votes, you were voting that my policy was the best. Whenever I was acquitted upon an indictment, it was a proof that my motion and proposals were according to law. Whenever you set your seal to my accounts at an audit, you confessed in addition that I had acted throughout with uprightness and integrity. And this being so, what epithet was it fitting or just that Ctesiphon should apply to my actions ? Was it not that which he saw applied by the People, and by juries on their oath, and ratified by Truth in the judgement of all men ?

'Yes,' he replies, 'but Cephalus'[n] boast was a noble 251 one—that he had never been indicted at all.' True, and a happy thing also it was for him.   But why should one who has often been tried, but has never been convicted of crime, deserve to incur criticism any the more on that account ? Yet in truth, men of Athens, so far as Aeschines is concerned, I too can make this noble boast that Cephalus made.   For he has never yet preferred or prosecuted any indictment against me ; so that by you at least, Aeschines, I am admitted to be no worse a citizen than Cephalus.

252   His want of feeling and his malignity may be seen in many ways, and not least in the remarks which he made about fortune.   For my part, I think that, as a rule, when one human being reproaches another with his fortune, he is a fool.   For when he who thinks himself most prosperous and fancies his fortune most excellent, does not know whether it will remain so until the evening, how can it be right to speak of one's fortune, or to taunt another with his ?   But since Aeschines adopts a tone of lofty superiority upon this as upon many other subjects, observe, men of Athens, how much more truthful and more becoming in a human being my own

253 remarks upon Aeschines' fortune will be.   I believe that the fortune of this city is good ; and I see that the God of Dodona also declares this to you through his oracle.   But I think that the prevailing fortune of mankind as a whole to-day is grievous and terrible.   For what man, Hellene or foreigner, has not tasted abundance of evil at this present

254 time ?   Now the fact that we chose the noblest course, and that we are actually better off than those Hellenes who expected to live in prosperity if they sacrificed us, I ascribe to the good fortune of the city.   But in so far as we failed, in so far as everything did not fall out in accordance with our wishes, I consider that the city has received the share

which was due to us of the fortune of mankind in general.
But my personal fortune, and that of every individual 255
among us, ought, I think, in fairness to be examined with
reference to our personal circumstances. That is my judgement with regard to fortune, and I believe (as I think you
also do) that my judgement is correct and just. But
Aeschines asserts that my personal fortune has more influence
than the fortune of the city as a community—the insignificant
and evil more than the good and important! How can
this be?

If, however, you determine at all costs to scrutinize my 256
fortune, Aeschines, then compare it with your own; and if
you find that mine is better than yours, then cease to revile
it. Examine it, then, from the very beginning. And, in
Heaven's name, let no one condemn me for any want of
good taste. For I neither regard one who speaks insultingly
of poverty, nor one who prides himself on having been
brought up in affluence, as a man of sense. But the slanders
and misrepresentations of this unfeeling man oblige me to
enter upon a discussion of this sort; and I will conduct
it with as much moderation as the facts allow.

I then, Aeschines, had the advantage as a boy of attending 257
the schools which became my position, and of possessing as
much as one who is to do nothing ignoble owing to poverty
must possess. When I passed out of boyhood, my life corre-
sponded with my upbringing—I provided choruses and
equipped warships; I paid the war-tax; I neglected none of
the paths to distinction in public or private life, but gave
my services both to my country and my friends; and when
I thought fit to enter public life, the measures which I
decided to adopt were of such a character that I have been

crowned many times both by my country and by many other Hellenic peoples, while not even you, my enemies, attempt to say that my choice was not at least an honourable
258 one. Such is the fortune which has accompanied my life, and though I might say much more about it, I refrain from doing so, in my anxiety not to annoy any one by the expression of my pride. And you—the lofty personage, the despiser of others—what has been your fortune when compared with this ?—the fortune, thanks to which you were brought up as a boy in the depths of indigence, in close attendance upon the school along with your father, pounding up the ink, sponging down the forms, sweeping the attendants' room,[n] occupying the position of a menial,
259 not of a free-born boy! Then, when you became a man, you used to read out the books[n] to your mother at her initiations, and help her in the rest of the hocus-pocus, by night dressing the initiated[n] in fawnskins, drenching them from the bowl, purifying them and wiping them down with the clay and the bran, and (when they were purified) bidding them stand up and say, ' The ill is done, the good begun,' priding yourself upon raising the shout of joy more loudly than any one had ever done before—and I can believe it, for, when his voice is so loud, you dare not imagine that
260 his shout is anything but superlatively fine. But by day you used to lead those noble companies through the streets, men crowned with fennel and white poplar,[n] throttling the puff-adders and waving them over your head, crying out ' Euoe, Saboe,'[n] and dancing to the tune of ' Hyes Attes, Attes Hyes '—addressed by the old hags as leader, captain, ivy-bearer, fan-bearer, and so on ; and as the reward of your services getting sops and twists and barley-bannocks ! Who

would not congratulate himself with good reason on such things, and bless his own fortune ? But when you were enrolled 261 among your fellow parishioners,[n] by whatever means (for of that I say nothing)—when, I say, you *were* enrolled, you at once selected the noblest of occupations, that of a clerk and servant to petty magistrates. And when at length you escaped from 262 this condition also, after yourself doing all that you impute to others, you in no way—Heaven knows !—disgraced your previous record by the life which you subsequently lived ; for you hired yourself out to the actors Simylus and Socrates— the Roarers, they were nicknamed—and played as a third-rate actor, collecting figs [n] and bunches of grapes and olives, like a fruiterer gathering from other peoples' farms, and getting more out of this than out of the dramatic competitions in which you were competing for your lives ; for there was war without truce or herald between yourselves and the specta- tors ; and the many wounds you received from them make it natural for you to jeer at the cowardice of those who have had no such experiences. But I will pass over all that might 263 be accounted for by your poverty, and proceed to my charges against your character itself. For you chose a line of political action (when at length it occurred to you to take up politics too), in pursuance of which, when your country's fortune was good, you lived the life of a hare, in fear and trembling, always expecting a thrashing for the crimes which lay on your conscience ; whereas all have seen your boldness amid the misfortunes of others. But 264 when a man plucks up courage at the death of a thousand of his fellow citizens, what does he deserve to suffer at the hands of the living ? I have much more to say about him, but I will leave it unsaid. It is not for me, I think, to mention lightly all the infamy and disgrace which I could prove to be connected with him, but only so much as it is not discreditable to myself to speak of.

265   And now review the history of your life and of mine, side by side—good temperedly, Aeschines, not unkindly : and then ask these gentlemen which fortune, of the two, each of them would choose. You taught letters ; I attended school. You conducted initiations ; I was initiated. You were a clerk ; I a member of the Assembly : you, a third-rate actor, I a spectator of the play. You used to be driven from the stage, while I hissed. Your political life has all been lived for the good of our enemies, mine for the good of my
266   country. To pass over all besides, even on this very day, I am being examined with regard to my qualification for a crown —it is already admitted that I am clear of all crimes ; while you have already the reputation of a dishonest informer, and for you the issue at stake is whether you are to continue such practices, or to be stopped once for all, through failing to obtain a fifth part of the votes. A good fortune indeed—can you not see ?—is that which has accompanied your life, that you should denounce mine !

267   And now let me read to you the evidence of the public burdens which I have undertaken ; and side by side with them, do you, Aeschines, read the speeches which you used to murder—

'I leave the abysm of death and gates of gloom,' [n]
and

'Know that I am not fain ill-news to bring';

and 'evil in evil wise ',[n] may you be brought to perdition, by the gods above all, and then by all those here present,

villainous citizen, villainous third-rate actor that you are.
(*To the clerk.*)   Read the evidence.

[*The evidence is read.*]

Such was I in my relation to the State. And as to my 268
private life, unless you all know that I was open-hearted and
generous and at the disposal of all who had need of me, I am
silent; I prefer to tell you nothing, and to produce no evidence
whatever, to show whether I ransomed some from the enemy,
or helped others to give their daughters in marriage, or
rendered any such services. For my principle may perhaps be 269
expressed thus. I think that one who has received a kindness ought to remember it all his life ; but that the doer of
the kindness should forget it once for all ; if the former is
to behave like a good man, the latter like one free from all
meanness. To be always recalling and speaking of one's
own benefactions is almost like upbraiding the recipients of
them. I will do nothing of the kind, and will not be led
into doing so. Whatever be the opinion that has been formed
of me in these respects, with that I am content.

But I desire to be rid of personal topics, and to say a little 270
more to you about public affairs. For if, Aeschines, you
can mention one of all those who dwell beneath the sun
above us, Hellene or foreigner, who has not suffered under
the absolute sway, first of Philip, and now of Alexander,
so be it ! I concede that it is my fortune or misfortune,
whichever you are pleased to call it, that has been to blame
for everything. But if many of those who have never once 271
even seen me or heard my voice have suffered much and
terribly—and not individuals alone, but whole cities and
nations—how much more just and truthful it is to regard

the common fortune (as it seems to be) of all mankind, and a certain stubborn drift of events in the wrong direction, 272 as the cause of these sufferings. Such considerations, however, you discard. You impute the blame to me, whose political life has been lived among my own fellow countrymen—and that, though you know that your slander falls in part (if not entirely) upon all of them, and above all upon yourself. For if, when I took part in the discussion of public affairs, I had had absolute power, it would have been possible for all of you, the other orators, to lay the blame 273 on me. But if you were present at every meeting of the Assembly; if the city always brought forward questions of policy for public consideration; if at the time my policy appeared the best to every one, and above all to you (for it was certainly from no goodwill that you relinquished to me the hopes, the admiration, the honours, which all attached themselves to my policy at that time, but obviously because the truth was too strong for you, and you had nothing better to propose); then surely you are guilty of monstrous iniquity, in finding fault to-day with a policy, than which, at the time, 274 you could propose nothing better. Among all the rest of mankind, I observe that some such principles as the following have been, as it were, determined and ordained. If a man commits a deliberate crime, indignation and punishment are ordained against him. If he commits an involuntary mistake, instead of punishment, he is to receive pardon. If, without crime or mistake, one who has given himself up wholly to that which seems to be for the advantage of all has, in company with all, failed to achieve success, then it is just, not to reproach or 275 revile such a man, but to sympathize with him. Moreover, it will be seen that all these principles are not so ordained in the laws alone. Nature herself has laid them down in her unwritten law, and in the moral consciousness of mankind. Aeschines, then, has so far surpassed all mankind in brutality and in the art of misrepresentation, that he actually denounces me for things which he himself mentioned under the name of misfortunes.

In addition to everything else, as though he had himself 276 always spoken straightforwardly and in loyalty, he bade you keep your eyes on me carefully, and make sure that I did not mislead or deceive you. He called me ' a clever speaker ', ' a wizard ', ' a sophist ', and so on : just as if it followed that when a man had the first word and attributed his own qualities to another, the truth was really as he stated, and his hearers would not inquire further who he himself was, that said such things. But I am sure that you all know this man, and are aware that these qualities belong to him far more than to me. And again, I am quite sure that my 277 cleverness—yes, let the word pass ; though I observe that the influence of a speaker depends for the most part on his audience ; for in proportion to the welcome and the good-will which you accord to each speaker is the credit which he obtains for wisdom ;—I am sure, I say, that if I too possess any such skill, you will all find it constantly fighting on your behalf in affairs of State, never in opposition to you, never for private ends ; while the skill of Aeschines, on the contrary, is employed, not only in upholding the cause of the enemy, but in attacking any one who has annoyed him or come into collision with him anywhere. He neither employs it uprightly, nor to promote the interests of the city. For 278 a good and honourable citizen ought not to require from a jury, who have come into court to represent the interests of the community, that they shall give their sanction to his anger, or his enmity, or any other such passion ; nor ought he to come before you to gratify such feelings. It were best that he had no such passions in his nature at all ; but if they are really inevitable, then he should keep them tame and subdued. Under what circumstances, then, should a politician and an orator show passion ? When any of the vital interests of his country are at stake ; when it is with its enemies that the People has to deal : those are the circumstances. For then is the opportunity of a loyal and

279 gallant citizen. But that when he has never to this day demanded my punishment, either in the name of the city or in his own, for any public—nor, I will add, for any private—crime, he should have come here with a trumped-up charge against the grant of a crown and a vote of thanks, and should have spent so many words upon it—that is a sign of personal enmity and jealousy and meanness, not of any good quality. And that he should further have discarded every form of lawsuit against myself, and should have come here to-day to attack the defendant, is the very extremity of

280 baseness. It shows, I think, Aeschines, that your motive in undertaking this suit was your desire, not to exact vengeance for any crime, but to give a display of rhetoric and elocution. Yet it is not his language, Aeschines, that deserves our esteem in an orator, nor the pitch of his voice, but his choice of the aims which the people chooses, his hatred or love of those whom his country loves or hates.

281 He whose heart is so disposed will always speak with loyal intent ; but he who serves those from whom the city foresees danger to herself, does not ride at the same anchor as the People, and therefore does not look for safety to the same

quarter. But I do, mark you ! For I have made the interests
of my countrymen my own, and have counted nothing as
reserved for my own private advantage. What ?   You 282
have not done so either ?   How can that be, when immediately after the battle you went your way as an ambassador
to Philip, the author of the calamities which befell your
country at that time ; and that, despite the fact that until
then you always denied this intimacy [n] with him, as every one
knows ?   But what is meant by a deceiver of the city ?   Is it
not one who does not say what he thinks ?   Upon whom does
the herald justly pronounce the curse ?   Is it not upon such
a man as this ?   With what greater crime can one charge
a man who is an orator, than that of saying one thing and
thinking another ?   Such a man you have been found to be. 283
And after this do you open your mouth, or dare to look
this audience in the face ?   Do you imagine that they do not
know who you are ?   or that the slumber of forgetfulness
has taken such hold upon them all, that they do not remember
the speeches which you used to deliver during the war, when
you declared with imprecations and oaths that you had nothing
to do with Philip, and that I was bringing this accusation
against you, when it was not true, to satisfy my personal
enmity?   But so soon as the news of the battle had come, 284
you thought no more of all this, but at once avowed and
professed that you stood on a footing of friendship and
guest-friendship with him ; though these were nothing but
your hireling-service under other names ; for upon what
honest or equal basis could Aeschines, the son of Glaucothea
the tambourine-player,[n] enjoy the guest-friendship, or the
friendship, or the acquaintance of Philip ?   I cannot see.
In fact, you had been hired by him to ruin the interests

of these your countrymen. And yet, though your own treason has been so plainly detected—though you have been an informer against yourself after the event—you still revile me, and reproach me with crimes of which, you will find, any one is more guilty than I.

285   Many a great and noble enterprise, Aeschines, did this city undertake and succeed in, inspired by me; and she did not forget them. It is a proof of this, that when, immediately after the event, the People had to elect one who should pronounce the oration over the dead, and you were nominated, they did not elect you, for all your fine voice, nor Demades, who had just negotiated the Peace, nor Hegemon,[n] nor any other member of your party: they elected me. And when you and Pythocles[n] came forward in a brutal and shameless fashion, God knows! and made the same charges against me as you are making again to-day, and abused me, the People elected me even more decidedly. And the reason you know

286 well; but I will tell it you nevertheless. They knew for themselves both the loyalty and zeal which inspired my conduct of affairs, and the iniquity of yourself and your friends. For what you denied with oaths when our cause was prosperous, you admitted in the hour of the city's failure; and those, accordingly, who were only enabled by the misfortunes of their country to express their views without fear, they decided to have been enemies of their own for a long while, though

287 only then did they stand revealed. And further, they thought that one who was to pronounce an oration over the dead, and to adorn their valour, should not have come beneath the same roof, nor shared the same libation,[n] as those who were arrayed against them; that he should not there join with those who with their own hands had slain them, in the

revel [n] and the triumph-song over the calamities of the
Hellenes, and then come home and receive honour—that he
should not play the mourner over their fate with his voice,
but should grieve for them in his heart. What they required
they saw in themselves and in me, but not in you ; and this
was why they appointed me, and not any of you. Nor, 288
when the people acted thus, did the fathers and brothers
of the slain, who were then publicly appointed to conduct
the funeral, act otherwise. For since (in accordance with
the ordinary custom) they had to hold the funeral-feast in
the house of the nearest of kin, as it were, to the slain,
they held it at my house, and with reason ; for though
by birth each was more nearly akin to his dead than I,
yet none stood nearer to them all in common. For he who
had their life and their success most at heart, had also, when
they had suffered what I would they had not, the greatest
share of sorrow for them all.

(*To the clerk*.) Read him the epitaph which the city 289
resolved to inscribe above them at the public cost ; (*to
Aeschines*) that even by these very lines, Aeschines, you may
know that you are a man destitute of feeling, a dishonest
accuser, an abominable wretch !

The Inscription.[n]

These for their country, fighting side by side,
By deeds of arms dispelled the foemen's pride.
Their lives they saved not, bidding Death make clear—
Impartial Judge !—their courage or their fear.
For Greece they fought, lest, 'neath the yoke brought low,
In thraldom she th' oppressor's scorn should know.

Now in the bosom of their fatherland
After their toil they rest—'tis God's command.
'Tis God's alone from failure free to live ; [n]
Escape from Fate to no man doth He give.

290   Do you hear, Aeschines [in these very lines], ' 'Tis God's
alone from failure free to live ' ? Not to the statesman has
he ascribed the power to secure success for those who strive,
but to the gods. Why then, accursed man, do you revile
me for our failure, in words which I pray the gods to turn
upon the heads of you and yours ?

291   But, even after all the other lying accusations which he
has brought against me, the thing which amazed me most of
all, men of Athens, was that when he mentioned what had
befallen the city, he did not think of it as a loyal and upright
citizen would have thought. He shed no tears ; he felt no
emotion of sorrow in his heart : he lifted up his voice, he
exulted, he strained his throat, evidently in the belief that
he was accusing me, though in truth he was giving us an
illustration, to his own discredit, of the utter difference
between his feelings and those of others, at the painful events
292 which had taken place.   But surely one who professes, as
Aeschines professes now, to care for the laws and the
constitution, ought to show, if nothing else, at least that he
feels the same griefs and the same joys as the People, and has
not, by his political profession, ranged himself on the side of
their opponents. That you have done the latter is manifest to-
day, when you pretend that the blame for everything is mine,
and that it is through me that the city was plunged in trouble:
though it was not through my statesmanship or my policy,
293 gentlemen, that you began to help the Hellenes : for were

you to grant me this—that it was through me that you had
resisted the dominion which was being established over the
Hellenes—you would have granted me a testimonial which
all those that you have given to others together could not
equal.   But neither would I make such an assertion; for it
would be unjust to you; nor, I am sure, would you concede
its truth: and if Aeschines were acting honestly, he would
not have been trying to deface and misrepresent the greatest
of your glories, in order to satisfy his hatred towards me.

But why do I rebuke him for this, when he has made 294
other lying charges against me, which are more outrageous
by far? For when a man charges me—I call Heaven and Earth
to witness!—with philippizing, what will he not say? By
Heracles and all the gods, if one had to inquire truthfully,
setting aside all calumny and all expression of animosity,
who are in reality the men upon whose heads all would
naturally and justly lay the blame for what has taken place,
you would find that it was those in each city who resemble
Aeschines, not those who resemble me.   For they, when 295
Philip's power was weak and quite insignificant—when we
repeatedly warned and exhorted you and showed you what
was best—they, to satisfy their own avarice, sacrificed the
interests of the community, each group deceiving and corrupting their own fellow citizens, until they brought them
into bondage. Thus the Thessalians were treated by Daochus,
Cineas, and Thrasydaeus;   the Arcadians by Cercidas,
Hieronymus and Eucampidas;   the Argives by Myrtis,
Teledamus, and Mnaseas;   the Eleans by Euxitheus, Cleo-
timus and Aristaechmus;   the Messenians by the sons of the
godforsaken Philiadas—Neon and Thrasylochus; the Sicy-
mians by Aristratus and Epichares;   the Corinthians by

Deinarchus and Demaretus; the Megareans by Ptoeodorus, Helixus and Perillus; the Thebans by Timolaus, Theogeiton, and Anemoetas; the Euboeans by Hipparchus and Sosi-
296 stratus. Daylight will fail me before the list of the traitors is complete. All these, men of Athens, are men who pursue the same designs in their own cities, as my opponents pursue among you—abominable men, flatterers, evil spirits, who have hacked the limbs each of his own fatherland, and like boon companions have pledged away their freedom, first to Philip and now to Alexander; men whose measure of happiness is their belly, and their lowest instincts; while as for freedom, and the refusal to acknowledge any man as lord—the standard and rule of good to the Hellenes of old—they have flung it to the ground.

297   Of this shameful and notorious conspiracy and wickedness—or rather (to speak with all earnestness, men of Athens), of this treason against the freedom of the Hellenes—Athens has been guiltless in the eyes of all men, in consequence of my states-manship, as I have been guiltless in your eyes. And do you then ask me for what merits I count myself worthy to receive honour? I tell you that at a time when every politician in Hellas had been corrupted—beginning with yourself—
298 [firstly by Philip, and now by Alexander], no opportunity that offered, no generous language, no grand promises, no hopes, no fears, nor any other motive, tempted or induced me to betray one jot of what I believed to be the rights and interests of the city; nor, of all the counsel that I have given to my fellow countrymen, up to this day, has any ever been given (as it has by you) with the scales of the mind inclining to the side of gain, but all out of an upright, honest, uncorrupted soul. I have taken the lead in greater affairs

than any man of my own time, and my administration has
been sound and honest throughout all. That is why I count 299
myself worthy of honour. But as for the fortifications and
entrenchments, for which you ridiculed me, I judge them
to be deserving, indeed, of gratitude and commendation—
assuredly they are so—but I set them far below my own
political services. Not with stones, nor with bricks, did
I fortify this city. Not such are the works upon which I
pride myself most. But would you inquire honestly wherein
my fortifications consist ? You will find them in munitions
of war, in cities, in countries, in harbours, in ships, in horses,
and in men ready to defend my fellow countrymen. These 300
are the defences I have set to protect Attica, so far as by
human calculation it could be done ; and with these I have
fortified our whole territory—not the circuit of the Peiraeus
or of the city alone. Nor in fact, did *I* prove inferior to
Philip in calculations—far from it ! —or in preparations for
war ; but the generals of the confederacy,[n] and their forces,
proved inferior to him in fortune. Where are the proofs
of these things ? They are clear and manifest. I bid you
consider them.

What was the duty of a loyal citizen—one who was acting 301
with all forethought and zeal and uprightness for his country's
good ? Was it not to make Euboea the bulwark of Attica
on the side of the sea, and Boeotia on that of the mainland,
and on that of the regions towards the Peloponnese, our
neighbours [n] in that direction ? Was it not to provide for
the corn-trade, and to ensure that it should pass along a continuously friendly coast all the way to the Peiraeus ? Was
it not to preserve the places which were ours—Procon- 302
nesus, the Chersonese, Tenedos—by dispatching expeditions

to aid them, and proposing and moving resolutions accordingly ; and to secure the friendship and alliance of the rest —Byzantium, Tenedos, Euboea ? Was it not to take away the greatest of the resources which the enemy possessed, and to add what was lacking to those of the city ? All this 303 has been accomplished by my decrees and by the measures which I have taken; and all these measures, men of Athens, will be found by any one who will examine them without jealousy, to have been correctly planned, and executed with entire honesty : the opportunity for each step was not, you will find, neglected or left unrecognized or thrown away by me, and nothing was left undone, which it was within the power and the reasoning capacity of a single man to effect. But if the might of some Divine Power, or the inferiority of our generals, or the wickedness of those who were betraying your cities, or all these things together, continuously injured our whole cause, until they effected its overthrow, how is 304 Demosthenes at fault ? Had there been in each of the cities of Hellas one man, such as I was, as I stood at my own post in your midst—nay, if all Thessaly and all Arcadia had each had but one man animated by the same spirit as myself—not one Hellenic people, either beyond or on this side of Thermopylae, would have experienced the evils which they now suffer. 305 All would have been dwelling in liberty and independence, free from all fears, secure and prosperous, each in their own land, rendering thanks for all these great blessings to you and the rest of the Athenian people, through me. But that you may know that in my anxiety to avoid jealousy, I am using language which is far from adequate to the actual facts, (*to the clerk*) read me this ; and take and recite the list of the expeditions sent out in accordance with my decrees.

[The list of expeditions is read.]

These measures, and others like them, Aeschines, were 306 the measures which it was the duty of a loyal and gallant citizen to take. If they were successful, it was certain that we should be indisputably the strongest power, and that with justice as well as in fact: and now that they have resulted otherwise, we are left with at least an honourable name. No man casts reproach either upon the city, or upon the choice which she made: they do but upbraid Fortune, who decided the issue thus. It was not, God knows, a citizen's duty to abandon 307 his country's interests, to sell his services to her opponents, and cherish the opportunities of the enemy instead of those of his country. Nor was it, on the one hand, to show his malice against the man who had faced the task of proposing and moving measures worthy of the city, and persisting in that intention; while, on the other hand, he remembered and kept his eyes fixed upon any private annoyance which another had caused him : nor was it to maintain a wicked and festering inactivity, as you so often do. Assuredly 308 there is an inactivity that is honest and brings good to the State—the inactivity which you,[n] the majority of the citizens, observe in all sincerity. But that is not the inactivity of Aeschines. Far from it ! He, on the contrary, retires just when he chooses, from public life (and he often chooses to do so), that he may watch for the moment when you will be sated with the continual speeches of the same adviser, or when fortune has thrown some obstacle in your path, or some other disagreeable event has happened (for in the life of man many things are possible) ; and then, when such an opportunity comes, suddenly, like a gale of wind, out of his retirement he comes forth an orator, with his voice in training, and his phrases and his sentences collected ; and these he strings together lucidly, without pausing for breath, though they bring with them no profit, no accession of anything good, but only calamity to one or another of his

309 fellow citizens, and shame to all alike. Surely, Aeschines, if all this practice and study sprang from an honest heart, resolved to pursue the interests of your country, the fruits of it should have been noble and honourable and profitable to all—alliances of cities, supplies of funds, opening of ports,[n] enactment of beneficial laws, acts of opposition to our proved enemies.

310 It was for all such services that men looked in bygone days ; and the past has offered, to any loyal and gallant citizen, abundant opportunities of displaying them : but nowhere in the ranks of such men will you ever be found to have stood—not first, nor second, nor third, nor fourth, nor fifth, nor sixth, nor in any position whatsoever ; at least, not in any matters whereby your country stood to gain.

311 For what alliance has the city gained by negotiations of yours ? What assistance, what fresh access of goodwill or fame ? What diplomatic or administrative action of yours has brought new dignity to the city ? What department of our home affairs, or our relations with Hellenic and foreign states, over which you have presided, has shown any improvement ? Where are your ships ? Where are your munitions of war ? Where are your dockyards ? Where are the walls that you have repaired ? Where are your cavalry ? Where in the world *is* your sphere of usefulness ? What pecuniary assistance have you ever given, as a good and generous fellow

312 citizen,[n] either to rich or poor ? ' But, my good sir,' you say, ' if I have done none of these things, I have at least given

my loyalty and goodwill.' Where? When? Why, even at
a time when all who ever opened their lips upon the platform
contributed voluntarily to save the city, till, last of all,
Aristonicus gave what he had collected to enable him to
regain his civil rights—even then, most iniquitous of men!
you never came forward or made any contribution whatever:
and assuredly it was not from poverty, when you had in-
herited more than five talents out of the estate of your
father-in-law Philo, and had received two talents subscribed
by the leaders of the Naval Boards,[n] for your damaging
attack upon my Naval Law.[n] But I will say no more about 313
this, lest by passing from subject to subject I should break
away from the matter in hand. It is at least plain that your
failure to contribute was not due to your poverty, but to
your anxiety to do nothing in opposition to those whose
interest is the guide of your whole public life. On what
occasions, then, do your spirit and your brilliancy show themselves? When something must be done to injure your
fellow countrymen—then your voice is most glorious, your
memory most perfect; then you are a prince of actors,
a Theocrines [n] on the tragic stage!

Again, you have recalled the gallant men of old, and you 314
do well to do so. Yet it is not just, men of Athens, to take
advantage of the good feeling which you may be relied upon
to entertain towards the dead, in order to examine me before
you by their standard, and compare me, who am still living
amongst you, with them. Who in all the world does not know 315
that against the living there is always more or less of secret
jealousy, while none, not even their enemies, hate the dead
any more? And am I, in spite of this law of nature, to
be judged and examined to-day by the standard of those

K

who were before me? By no means! It would be neither just nor fair, Aeschines. But let me be compared with yourself, or with any of those who have adopted the same
316 policy as yourself, and are still alive. And consider this also. Which of these alternatives is the more honourable? Which is better for the city?—that the good services done by men of former times—tremendous, nay even beyond all description though they may be—should be made an excuse for exposing to ingratitude and contumely those that are rendered to the present generation? or that all who act in loyalty should have a share in the honours and the kindness
317 which our fellow citizens dispense? Aye, and (if I must say this after all) the policy and the principles which I have adopted will be found, if rightly viewed, to resemble and to have the same aims as those of the men who in that age received praise; while yours resemble those of the dishonest assailants of such persons in those days. For in their time also there were obviously persons who disparaged the living and praised the men of old, acting in the same malicious way
318 as yourself. Do you say then, that I am in no way like them? But are *you* like them, Aeschines? or your brother? or any other orator of the present day? For my part, I should say, 'None.' Nay, my good sir—to use no other epithet— compare the living with the living, their contemporaries, as men do in every other matter, whether they are comparing poets or choruses or competitors in the games.
319 Because Philammon was not so powerful as Glaucus of Carystus [n] and some other athletes of former times, he did not leave Olympia uncrowned: but because he fought better than all who entered against him, he was crowned and proclaimed victor. Do you likewise examine me beside the

orators of the day—beside yourself, beside any one in the
world that you choose. I fear no man's rivalry. For, while 320
the city was still free to choose the best course, and all alike
could compete with one another in loyalty to their country, I
was found the best adviser of them all. It was by my laws, by
my decrees, by my diplomacy, that all was effected. Not one
of your party appeared anywhere, unless some insult was to
be offered to your fellow countrymen. But when there
happened, what I would had never happened—when it
was not statesmen that were called to the front, but those
who would do the bidding of a master, those who were
anxious to earn wages by injuring their country, and to flatter
a stranger—then, along with every member of your party,
you were found at your post, the grand and resplendent owner
of a stud ; [n] while I was weak, I confess, yet more loyal to my
fellow countrymen than you. Two characteristics, men of 321
Athens, a citizen of a respectable character (for this is perhaps
the least invidious phrase that I can apply to myself) must
be able to show : when he enjoys authority, he must maintain
to the end the policy whose aims are noble action and the
pre-eminence of his country : and at all times and in every
phase of fortune he must remain loyal. For this depends
upon his own nature ; while his power and his influence are
determined by external causes. And in me, you will find, this
loyalty has persisted unalloyed. For mark this. Not when 322
my surrender was demanded, not when I was called to
account before the Amphictyons, not in face either of threats
or of promises, not when these accursed men were hounded
on against me like wild beasts, have I ever been false to my
loyalty towards you. For from the very first, I chose the
straight and honest path in public life : I chose to foster

the honour, the supremacy, the good name of my country,
323 to seek to enhance them, and to stand or fall with them. I do
not walk through the market, cheerful and exultant over
the success of strangers, holding out my hand and giving the
good tidings to any whom I expect to report my conduct
yonder, but shuddering, groaning, bowing myself to the
earth, when I hear of the city's good fortune, as do these
impious men, who make a mock of the city—not remembering
that in so doing they are mocking themselves—while they
direct their gaze abroad, and, whenever another has gained
success through the failure of the Hellenes, belaud that state
of things, and declare that we must see that it endures for
all time.

324　Never, O all ye gods, may any of you consent to their
desire! If it can be, may you implant even in these men
a better mind and heart. But if they are verily beyond all
cure, then bring them and them alone to utter and early
destruction, by land and sea. And to us who remain, grant
the speediest release from the fears that hang over us, and
safety that naught can shake!

NOTES

ON THE NAVAL BOARDS

§ 1. *who praise your forefathers.* The advocates of war with Persia had doubtless appealed to the memory of Marathon and Salamis, and the old position of Athens as the champion of Greece against Persia.

§ 10, 11. The argument is this : ' If a war with Persia needed a special kind of force, we could not prepare for it without being detected : but as all wars need the same kind of force, our preparations need rouse no suspicion in Persia particularly.'

acknowledged foes : i.e. probably Thebes, or the revolted allies of Athens, with whom a disadvantageous peace had, perhaps, just been made. It is not, however, impossible that Philip also is in the orator's mind ; for though at the time he was probably engaged in war with the Illyrians and Paeonians, his quarrel with Athens in regard to Amphipolis had not been settled. The Olynthians may also be thought of. (See Introd. to Phil. I and Olynthiacs.)

§ 12. *rhapsodies.* The rhapsodes who went about Greece reciting Homer and other poets had lost the distinction they once enjoyed, and 'rhapsody' became a synonym for idle declamation.

§ 14. *a bold speech* : i.e. a demand for instant war, helped out by rhetorical praises of the men of old.

§ 16. *unmarried heiresses and orphans.* These would be incapable of discharging the duties of the trierarchy, though their estates were liable for the war-tax. Partners were probably exempted, when none of them possessed so large a share in the common property as would render him liable for trierarchy.

property outside Attica. According to the terms made by Athens with her allies when the ' Second Delian League ' was formed in 378, Athens undertook that no Athenian should hold property in an allied State. But this condition had been broken, and the multiplication of Athenian estates (κληρουχίαι) in allied territories had been one of the causes of the war with the allies.

unable to contribute : e.g. owing to no longer possessing the estate which he had when the assessment was made.

§ 17. *to associate*, &c. The sections which contained a very rich man were to have poor men included in it, so that the total wealth of every section might be the same, and the distribution of the burden between the sections fair.

§ 18. *the first hundred*, &c. Demosthenes thinks of the fleet as composed, according to need, of 100, 200, or 300 vessels, and treats each hundred as a separate squadron, to be separately divided among the Boards.

by lot. In this and other clauses of his proposal, Demosthenes stipulates for the use of the lot (συγκληρῶσαι, ἐπικληρῶσαι) to avoid all unfair selection. It is only in the distribution of duties among the smaller sections within each Board that assignment by arrangement (ἀποδοῦναι, a word suggesting distribution according to fitness or convenience) is to be allowed.

§ 19. *taxable capital* (τίμημα). The war-tax and the trierarchic burdens were assessed on a valuation of the contributor's property. Upon this valuation he paid the percentage required. (The old view that he was taxed not upon his capital, as valued, but upon a fraction of it varying with his wealth, rests upon an interpretation of passages in the Speeches against Aphobus, which is open to grave question.) The total amount of the single valuations was the 'estimated taxable capital of the country' (τίμημα τῆς χώρας). This, in the case of the trierarchy, would be the aggregate amount of the valuations of the 1,200 wealthiest men, viz. 6,000 talents. (Of course the capital taxable for the war-tax would be considerably larger. Even at a time when the prosperity of Attica was much lower, in 378–377 B.C., it was nearly 6,000 talents, according to Polybius, ii. 62. 6.)

§ 20. A tabular statement will make this plain :—

Ships.	Persons responsible.	Total capital taxable for each ship.
100	12	60 tal.
200	6	30 ,,
300	4	20 ,,

The percentage payable on the taxable capital was of course higher, the larger the number of ships required. Each ship appears to have cost on the average a talent to equip. The percentages in the three cases contained in the table would therefore be $1\frac{2}{3}$, $3\frac{1}{3}$, and 5, respectively. (Compare § 27.)

§ 21. *fittings . . . in arrear.* Apparently former trierarchs had not always given back the fittings of their vessels, which had either been provided at the expense of the State, or lent to the trierarchs by the State.

§ 23. *wards* (τριττύες). The trittys or ward was one-third of a tribe.

§ 25. *you see . . . city.* The Assembly met on the Pnyx, whence there was a view of the Acropolis and of the greater part of the ancient city.

prophets. The Athenian populace seems always to have been liable to the influence of soothsayers, who professed to utter oracles from the gods, particularly when war was threatening. This was so (e. g.) at the time of the Peloponnesian War (Thucyd. ii. 8, v. 26), and the soothsayer is delightfully caricatured by Aristophanes in the *Birds* and elsewhere.

§ 29. *two hundred ships . . . one hundred were Athenian.* In the Speech on the Crown, § 238, Demosthenes gives the numbers as 300 and 200. Perhaps a transcriber at an early stage in the history of the text accidentally wrote HH (the symbol for 200) instead of HHH, in the case of the first number, and a later scribe then 'corrected' the second number into H instead of HH. The numbers given by Herodotus are 378 and 180, and, for the Persian ships, 1,207.

§ 31. *against Egypt*, which was now in rebellion against Artaxerxes. Orontas, Satrap of Mysia, was more or less constantly in revolt during this period.

§ 32. *even more certainly* (πάλαι) : lit. 'long ago'. The transition from temporal to logical priority is paralleled in certain uses of other temporal adverbs, e. g. εὐθύς (Aristotle, *Poet.* v), and σχολῇ (of which, as Weil notes, πάλαι is the exact opposite).

§ 34. *sins against Hellas.* This refers to the support given to the Persian invaders by Thebes in the Persian Wars (Herod. viii. 34).

FOR THE MEGALOPOLITANS

§ 4. *Plataeae* (which had been overthrown by the enemies of Athens in the course of the Peloponnesian War, but rebuilt, with the aid of Sparta, in 378) was destroyed by Thebes in 373–372. About the same time Thebes destroyed Thespiae, which, like Plataeae, was well-disposed towards Athens ; and in 370 the Thebans massacred the male population of Orchomenus, and sold the women and children into slavery.

§ 11. *Oropus* had sometimes belonged to Thebes and sometimes to Athens. In 366 it was taken from Athens by Themison, tyrant of Eretria (exactly opposite Oropus, on the coast of Euboea), and placed in the hands of Thebes until the ownership should be decided. Thebes retained it until it was restored to Athens by Philip in 338.

§ 12. *when all the Peloponnesians*, &c. The reference seems to be to the year 370, shortly after the battle of Leuctra, when the Peloponnesian States sought the protection of Athens against Sparta, and, being refused, became allies of Thebes (Diodorus xv. 62). In 369 Athens made an alliance with Sparta.

§ 14. *saved the Spartans.* See last note. Athens also assisted the Spartans at Mantineia in 362.

the Thebans. In 378 and the following years Athens assisted Thebes against the Spartans under Agesilaus and Cleombrotus.

the Euboeans. In 358 or 357 Euboea succeeded in obtaining

freedom from the domination of Thebes by the aid of Athenian troops under Timotheus.

§ 16. *Triphylia*, a district between Elis and Messenia, was the subject of a long-standing dispute between the Eleans and the Arcadians, and seems to have been in the hands of the latter since (about) 368.

Tricaranum, a fortress in the territory of Phlius, had been seized by the Argives in 369, and used as a centre from which incursions were made into Phliasian territory.

§ 20. *allies of Thebes* : in order to preserve the balance of power between Thebes and Sparta.

§ 21. *the Theban confederacy*. The reference is particularly to the Arcadian allies of Thebes, but the wider expression perhaps suggests a general policy of a more ambitious kind.

§ 22. *you, I think, know.* He refers to the older members of the Assembly, who would remember the tyrannical conduct of Sparta during the period of her supremacy (the first quarter of the fourth century B.C.).

§ 27. *pillars*. The terms of an alliance were usually recorded upon pillars erected by each State on some site fixed by agreement or custom.

§ 28. *in the war* : i. e. the ' Sacred War ', against the Phocians.

FOR THE FREEDOM OF THE RHODIANS

§ 3. *now it will be seen* : i. e. if you come to a right decision, and help the Rhodians.

§ 5. *the Egyptians.* See Speech on Naval Boards, § 31 n.

§ 6. *to advise you* : i. e. in the Speech on the Naval Boards (see especially §§ 10, 11 of that Speech).

§ 9. *Ariobarzanes*, Satrap of the Hellespont, joined in the general revolt of the princes of Asia Minor against Persia in 362, at first secretly (as though making war against other satraps) but afterwards openly. Timotheus was sent to help him, on the understanding that he must not break the Peace of Antalcidas

(378 B.C.), according to which the Greek cities in Asia were to belong to the king, but the rest were to be independent (except that Athens was to retain Lemnos, Imbros, and Scyros). When Ariobarzanes broke out in open revolt, Timotheus could not help him without breaking the first provision; but the Persian occupation of Samos was itself a violation of the second, and he was therefore justified in relieving the town.

§ 11. *while he is in her neighbourhood.* Artaxerxes almost certainly went in person to Egypt about this time. (That he went before 346 is proved by Isocrates, *Philippus*, § 101; and he was no doubt expected to go, even before he went.) The alternative rendering, 'since he is still to be a neighbouring power to herself,' is less good, since he would be this, whether he conquered Egypt or not.

§ 14. *Rhodians who are now in possession*: i.e. the oligarchs, who held the town with the help of Caria.

some of their fellow-citizens: i.e. some of the democratic party.

§ 15. *official patron* (πρόξενος). The 'official patron' of another State in Athens was necessarily an Athenian, and so differed from the modern consul, whom he otherwise resembled in many ways (cf. Phillipson, *International Law and Custom of Ancient Greece and Rome*, vol. i, pp. 147–56).

§ 17. *publicly provided*: i.e. in treaties between the States.

§ 22. *when our democracy*, &c.: i.e. in 404, when, at the conclusion of the Peloponnesian War, the tyranny of the Thirty was established, and a very large number of democratic citizens were driven into exile. The Argives refused the Spartan demand for the surrender of some of these to the Thirty (Diodorus xiv. 6).

§ 23. *one who is a barbarian—aye, and a woman* (βάρβαρον ἄνθρωπον καὶ ταῦτα γυναῖκα). This has been taken to refer (1) to Artaxerxes and Artemisia. But καὶ ταῦτα cannot be simply πρὸς τούτῳ, and καὶ ταῦτα γυναῖκα must refer to the same person as βάρβαρον ἄνθρωπον; (2) to Artaxerxes alone, the words καὶ ταῦτα γυναῖκα being a gratuitous insult such as it was customary for Athenians to level at any Persian; (3) to Artemisia alone, ἄνθρωπος being feminine here as often. It is not possible to decide certainly between (2) and (3). Artemisia is more prominent in the speech than the king, but it is the king who is referred to in the next sentence.

§ 24. *rendered Athens weak.* The success of Sparta in the Peloponnesian War was rendered possible, to a great extent, by the supply of funds from Persia. In 401 Cyrus made his famous expedition against Artaxerxes II, and Clearchus (with other generals) commanded the Greek troops which assisted him. The death of Cyrus in the battle of Cunaxa in 401 put an end to his rebellion.

§ 25. *rights of the rest of the world.* Weil suggests that it may have been argued that to intervene in Rhodian affairs would be to break the treaty made with the allies in 355 (about), at the end of the Social War, whereby their independence was guaranteed.

§ 26. *Chalcedon* was on the Asiatic shore of the Bosporus, and therefore by the Peace of Antalcidas belonged to the king (see n. on § 9). By the same treaty, Selymbria, on the north coast of the Propontis, ought to have been independent. The Byzantines, who had obtained their independence of Athens in the Social War, were extending their influence greatly at this time.

§ 27. *the treaty*: again the Peace of Antalcidas.

even if there actually are such advisers: or, ' even if any one actually asserts the existence of such persons.'

§ 29. *two treaties.* The first must be the Peace of Callias (444 B.C.), the terms of which are given in the Speech on the Embassy, § 273. The second was the Peace of Antalcidas.

§ 30. *the knowledge of what is right.* The parallel passage in § 1 seems to confirm this rendering, rather than the alternative, ' the intention to do what is right.'

§ 33. *oligarchical.* This expression is partly directed at those who, in opposing the exiled democrats, supported the oligarchs of Rhodes ; and it may be partly explained by the fact that the policy of Eubulus, who wished to avoid all interferences which might lead to war, was particularly satisfactory to the wealthier classes in Athens. But it was a common practice to accuse an opponent of anti-democratic sentiments, and of trying to get the better of the people by illegitimate means (cf. Speech on Embassy, § 314, &c.).

§ 35. Cf. Speech on Naval Boards, § 41.

THE FIRST PHILIPPIC

§ 3. *the war with Sparta.* Probably the Boeotian War (378–371 B.C.), when Athens supported Thebes against Sparta.

in defence of the right. The attempt of the Spartans to conquer Boeotia was a violation of the Peace of Antalcidas (see n. on Speech for Rhodians, § 6). But Demosthenes' expression may be quite general in its meaning.

§ 4. *tribes.* Probably refers especially to the Thracians (see Introd. to the Speech). The Paeonian and Illyrian chieftains also made alliance with Athens in 356.

§ 17. *to Euboea.* See Speech for Megalopolitans, § 14 n.

to Haliartus : in 395, when Athens sent a force to aid the Thebans against the Spartans under Lysander. (For other allusions see Introd. to the Speech.)

§ 19. *paper-armies* (ἐπιστολιμαίους ... δυνάμεις) : lit. ' armies existing in dispatches.'

§ 24. *Athens once maintained,* &c. The reference is to the Corinthian war of 394–387 B.C. The Athenian general Iphicrates organized a mercenary force of peltasts in support of Corinth, and did great damage to Sparta ; he was succeeded in the command by Chabrias. Nothing more is certainly known of Polystratus than is told us here, though he may be referred to in the Speech against Leptines, § 84, as receiving honours from Athens.

to Artabazus. In 356 Chares was sent to oppose the revolted allies of Athens, but being short of funds, assisted Artabazus in his rebellion against Persia, and was richly rewarded. (See Introd. to Speech on Naval Boards.)

§ 25. *spectators of these mysteries of generalship* (ἐπόπται τῶν στρατηγουμένων). The word ἐπόπτης is chiefly used of spectators of the mysteries, and is here applied sarcastically to the citizens whom Demosthenes desires to see what has hitherto been a hidden thing from them—the conduct of their generals.

§ 26. *ten captains and generals*, &c. There was one general (στρατηγός) and one captain (ταξίαρχος) of infantry, and one general of cavalry (φύλαρχος), for each of the ten tribes. There were two regular masters of the horse (ἵππαρχοι), and a third appointed for the special command of the Athenian troops in Lemnos. The generals (στρατηγοί) had various civil duties, among them the organization of the military processions at the Panathenaea and other great festivals.

§ 27. *Menelaus*. Either a Macedonian chieftain, who had assisted the Athenian commander Timotheus against Poteidaea in 364, and probably received Athenian citizenship; or else Philip's half-brother Menelaus. But there is no evidence that the latter ever served in the Athenian forces, and probably the former is meant.

§ 31. *Etesian winds*. These blow strongly from the north over the Aegean from July to September.

§ 33. *the whole force in its entirety*. So with Butcher's punctuation. But it is perhaps better to place a comma after δύναμιν, and translate, ' after making ready . . . soldiers, ships, cavalry—the entire force complete—you bind them,' &c.

§ 34. See Introd. to the Speech. Geraestus was the southernmost point of Euboea. The ' sacred trireme ', the Paralus, when conveying the Athenian deputation to the Festival of Delos, put in on its way at Marathon, where there was an altar of the Delian Apollo, to offer sacrifice.

§ 35. The festival of the Panathenaea was managed by the Athlothetae, who were appointed by lot, and consequently could not be specially qualified; whereas the stewards (ἐπιμεληταί) who assisted the Archon in the management of the Dionysia, were at this time elected, presumably on the ground of their fitness.

an amount of trouble (ὄχλον). Possibly 'a larger crowd'. But there is no point in mentioning the crowd; the point lies in the pains taken; and Thucyd. vi. 24 (ὑπὸ τοῦ ὀχλώδους τῆς παρασκευῆς) confirms the rendering given.

§ 36. The choregus paid the expenses of a chorus at the Dionysiac (and certain other) festivals. The gymnasiarchs, or stewards of the games, managed the games and torch-races which formed part of the Panathenaea and many other festivals. The offices were imposed by law upon men who possessed a certain estate, but any one who felt that another could bear the burden better might challenge him either to perform the duty or to exchange property with him. (See Appendix to Goodwin's edition of Demosthenes' Speech against Meidias.)

independent freedmen: lit. 'dwellers apart,' i.e. freedmen who no longer lived with the master whose slaves they had been.

§ 43. *empty ships.* If these are the ships referred to in Olynth. III, § 4, the date of the First Philippic must be later than October 351 B.C.

§ 46. *promises.* The 'promises of Chares' became almost proverbial.

§ 47. *examination*, or 'audit'. A general, like every other responsible official, had to report his proceedings, at the end of his term of office, to a Board of Auditors, and might be prosecuted before a jury by any one who was dissatisfied with his report.

§ 48. *negotiating with Sparta*, &c. As a matter of fact, Philip had evidently come to an understanding with Thebes by this time; but he may have caused some such rumours to be spread, in order to get rid of any possible opposition from Sparta. The 'breaking-up of the free states' probably refers to the desire of Sparta to destroy Megalopolis, which was in alliance with Thebes.

sent ambassadors to the king. Arrian, ii. 14, mentions a letter of Darius to Alexander, recalling how Philip had been in friendship and alliance with Artaxerxes Ochus. It is possible, therefore, that the rumour to which Demosthenes alludes had some foundation.

THE FIRST OLYNTHIAC

(*Note.*—Most of the allusions in the Olynthiacs are explained by the Introduction to the First Philippic.)

§ 4. *power over everything, open or secret.* The translation generally approved, ' power to publish or conceal his designs,' is hardly possible. The καί in the phrase ῥητὰ καὶ ἀπόρρητα (or ἄρρητα) cannot be taken disjunctively here, when it is always conjunctive in this phrase elsewhere, the whole phrase being virtually equivalent to ' everything whatever '.

§ 5. *how he treated,* &c. The scholiast says that Philip killed the traitors at Amphipolis first, saying that if they had not been faithful to their own countrymen, they were not likely to be faithful to himself ; and that the traitors at Pydna, finding that they were not likely to be spared, took sanctuary, and having been persuaded to surrender themselves on promise of their lives, were executed nevertheless. Neither story is confirmed by other evidence.

§ 8. *in aid of the Euboeans* : in 358 or 357. See Speech for Megalopolitans, § 14 n.

§ 13. *Magnesia.* There seems to have been a town of the same name as the district.

attacked the Olynthians. This refers to the short invasion of 351 (see vol. i, p. 70), not to that which is the subject of the Olynthiacs.

Arybbas was King of the Molossi, and uncle of Philip's wife, Olympias. Nothing is known of this expedition against him. He was deposed by Philip in 343. (See vol. ii, p. 3.)

§ 17. *these towns* : the towns of the Chalcidic peninsula, over which Olynthus had acquired influence. This sentence shows that Olynthus itself had not yet been attacked.

§ 26. *But, my good Sir,* &c. This must be the objection of an imaginary opponent. It can hardly be taken (as seems to be intended by Butcher) as Demosthenes' reply to the question, ' Or some other power ? ' (' But, my good Sir, the other power will

not want to help him.') There is, however, much to be said for
Sandys's punctuation, ἐὰν μὴ βοηθήσηθ' ὑμεῖς ἢ ἄλλος τις, 'unless
you or some other power go to their aid.' After the death of
Onomarchus in 352, the Phocians were incapable of withstanding
invasion without help.

THE SECOND OLYNTHIAC

§ 14. *Timotheus*, &c. In 364 an Athenian force under
Timotheus invaded the territory of the Olynthian League, and
took Torone, Poteidaea, and other towns, with the help of
Perdiccas, King of Macedonia.

ruling dynasty: i. e. the dynasty of Lycophron and Peitholaus
at Pherae. (See Introd. to First Philippic.)

§ 28. *this war*: i. e. the war with Philip generally. The
reference is supposed to be to the conduct of Chares in 356 (cf.
Phil. I, § 24 n.), though in fact it was against the revolted allies,
not against Philip, that he had been sent. Sigeum was a favourite
resort of Chares, and it is conjectured that he may have obtained
possession of Lampsacus and Sigeum (both on the Asiatic shore
of the Hellespont) in 356. The explanation of the conduct of the
generals is to be found in the fact that in Asia Minor they could
freely appropriate prizes of war and plunder, since under the
terms of the Peace of Antalcidas, Athens could claim nothing in
Asia for her own.

§ 29. *taxes by Boards*. Each of the Boards constituted in
378–377 for the collection of the war-tax (see vol. i, p. 31) had a
leader or chairman (ἡγεμών), one of the 300 richest men in Athens,
whose duty it was to advance the sums required by the State,
recovering them afterwards from the other members of the Boards.
Probably the Three Hundred were divided equally among the
100 Boards, a leader, a 'second', and a 'third' (Speech on
Crown, § 103) being assigned to each. The 'general' here perhaps
corresponds to the 'second'.

THE THIRD OLYNTHIAC

§ 4. *two or three years ago* (lit. ' this is the third or fourth year since). It was in November 352 B.C. If the present Speech was delivered before November 349, not quite three years would have elapsed. (The Greek words, τρίτον ἢ τέταρτον ἔτος τουτί, must, on the analogy of the Speech against Meidias, § 13, against Stephanus, II. § 13, and against Aphobus, I. § 24, &c., mean ' two or three ', not ' three or four years ago '). The vagueness of the expression is more likely to be due to the date of the Third Olynthiac being not far short of three years from that of the siege of Heraeon Teichos, than to the double-dating (on the one hand by actual lapse of time, and on the other by archon-years—from July to July—or by military campaigning seasons) which most commentators assume to be intended here, but which seems to be over-subtle and unlike Demosthenes.

that year : i.e. the archonship of Aristodemus, which ran from July 352 B.C. to July 351.

§ 5. *the mysteries.* These were celebrated from the 14th to the 27th of Boedromion (late in September).

Charidemus, of Oreus in Euboea, was a mercenary leader who had served many masters at different times—Athens, Olynthus, Cotys, and Cersobleptes—and had played most of them false at some time or other. But he was given the citizenship in 357 for the part which he had taken in effecting the cession of the Chersonese to Athens, and was a favourite with the people. He was sent on the occasion here referred to with ten ships, for which he was to find mercenary soldiers.

§ 6. *with might . . . power.* A quotation, probably from the text of the treaty of alliance between Athens and Olynthus.

§ 8. *funds of the Phocians are exhausted.* The Phocian leader Phalaecus had been using the temple-treasures of Delphi, but they were now exhausted.

§ 10. *a Legislative Commission* : i.e. a Special Commission on the model of the regular Commission which was appointed annually from the jurors for the year (if the Assembly so decreed), and before which those who wished to make or to oppose changes in the laws appeared, the proceedings taking the form of a prosecution and defence of the laws in question. The Assembly itself did not legislate, though it passed decrees, which had to be consistent with the existing laws. As regards legislation, it merely decided whether in any given year alterations in the laws should or should not be allowed.

§ 11. *malingerers.* The scholiast says that the choregi were persuaded to choose persons as members of their choruses, in order to enable them to escape military service, choreutae being legally exempted. Other exemptions also existed.

§ 12. *persons who proposed them.* This can only refer to Eubulus and his party.

§ 20. *Corinthians and Megareans.* From the pseudo-Demosthenic Speech on the Constitution (περὶ συντάξεως) and from Philochorus (quoted in the Scholia of Didymus upon that Speech) it appears that the Athenians had in 350 invaded Megara, under the general Ephialtes, and forced the Megareans to agree to a delimitation of certain land sacred to the two goddesses of Eleusis, which the Megareans had violated, perhaps for some years past (see Speech against Aristocrates, § 212). A scholiast also refers to the omission by Corinth to invite the Athenians to the Isthmian games, in consequence of which the Athenians sent an armed force to attend the games. Probably this was also a recent occurrence, and due to an understanding between Corinth and Megara.

§ 21. *my own namesake*: i.e. Demosthenes, who was a distinguished general during the Peloponnesian War, and perished in the Sicilian expedition.

§ 24. *for forty-five years*: i.e. between the Persian and Peloponnesian Wars, 476–431 B.C.

the king: i.e. Perdiccas II, who, however, took the side of Sparta shortly after the beginning of the Peloponnesian War. He died in 413. (The date of the beginning of his reign is unknown, but he did not become sole king of the whole of Macedonia until 436.)

§ 27. *Spartans had been ruined* : sc. by the battles of Leuctra (in 371) and Mantineia (in 362).

Thebans had their hands full, owing to the war with the Phocians, from 356 onwards.

§ 28. *in the war*, when Athens joined Thebes against Sparta (in 378). ' The allies' are those members of the Second Delian League (formed in 378) who had been lost in the Social War which ended in or about 355, when Athens was at peace with Thebes and Sparta.   (See Introduction, vol. i, p. 9.)

§ 31. *procession at the Boedromia*. The Boedromia was a festival held in September in honour of Apollo and Artemis Agrotera. Probably a procession was not a regular part of the festival at this time. The importance which the populace attached to such processions is illustrated by the Speech against Timocrates, § 161.

§ 34. *is it then paid service*, &c. : almost, ' do you then suggest that we should *earn* our money ? '

§ 35. *adding or subtracting* : sc. from the sums dispensed by the State to the citizens.

somebody's mercenaries. The reference is probably to the successes of Charidemus when first sent (see Introd. to Olynthiacs).

ON THE PEACE

5. *disturbances in Euboea*. Plutarchus of Eretria applied for Athenian aid against Callias of Chalcis, who was attacking him with the aid of Macedonian troops. Demosthenes was strongly opposed to granting the request, but it was supported by Eubulus and Meidias, and a force was sent under Phocion, probably early in 348 (though the chronology has been much debated, and some place the expedition in 350 or 349). Owing to the premature action or the treachery of Plutarchus at Tamynae (where the Athenian army was attacked), Phocion had some difficulty in winning a victory. Plutarchus afterwards seized a number of Athenian soldiers, and Athens had actually to

ransom them. Phocion's successor, Molossus, was unsuccessful. When peace was made in the summer of 348, the Euboeans became for the most part independent of Athens, and were regarded with ill-feeling by Athens for some years. There is no proof that the proposers of the expedition were bribed, as Demosthenes alleges.

§ 6. *Neoptolemus.* See Speech on Embassy, §§ 12, 315.

§ 8. *public service* : i.e. as trierarch or choregus or gymnasiarch, &c. See n. on Phil. I. § 36.

§ 10. *there were some* : i.e. Aeschines and his colleagues. (See Introd.)

Thespiae and Plataeae. See Speech for Megalopolitans, § 4 n.

§ 14. *self-styled Amphictyons.* The Amphictyonic Council represented the ancient Amphictyonic League of Hellenic tribes (now differing widely in importance, but equally represented on the Council), and was supreme in all matters affecting the Temple of Apollo at Delphi. (See n. on Speech on Crown, § 148.) The Council summoned by Philip was open to criticism (1) because only certain members of it were present, of whom the Thebans and Thessalians were the chief, (2) because Philip had been given the vote of the dispossessed Phocians.

§ 15. *however stupid*, &c. It had been conventional for over a century to apply this adjective to the Boeotians, and therefore to the Thebans. For a more favourable view, see W. Rhys Roberts, *Ancient Boeotians*, chap. i.

§ 16. *Oropus.* See Speech for Megalopolitans, § 11 n.

§ 18. *Argives*, &c. See Speech for Megalopolitans throughout with Introd.).

those whom they have exiled : especially the refugees from Orchomenus and Coroneia. See vol. i, p. 124.

Phocian fugitives. The Amphictyonic Council had recently declared that these had been guilty of sacrilege, and might be seized wherever they might be.

§ 20. *all that they themselves had toiled for* : i.e. the conquest of the Phocians in the Sacred War.

§ 22. *some persons* : i.e. Aeschines and others who tried to excuse Philip's treatment of the Phocians to the Athenian people.

§ 23. *admission ... Delphi.* The Phocians had formerly contrived their exclusion from the Amphictyonic meeting and from the temple and oracle of Delphi. The Council now restored them, and excluded the Phocians.

§ 24. *refuse to submit* : reading ⟨οὐδ'⟩ ὁτιοῦν ὑπομεῖναι. The insertion of οὐδέ (after Cobet) seems necessary. ὁτιοῦν ὑπομεῖναι alone would mean 'face any risk', but this would be contradicted by the next clause. To translate, 'who think that we should face any risk, but do not see that the risk would be one of war,' is to narrow the meaning of ὁτιοῦν unduly.

§ 25. *Treaty of Peace* : i.e. the Peace of Philocrates.

Cardians. The Athenians claimed Cardia (the key of the Chersonese on the Thracian side) as an ally, though in fact it was expressly excluded from the towns ceded to Athens by Cersobleptes in 357, and had made alliance with Philip in 352.

prince of Caria. See Speech for Rhodians (with Introd.).

drive our vessels to shore : a regular form of ancient piracy (see Speech on Chersonese, § 28). The Byzantines drove the Athenian corn-ships into their own harbour. The victims were relieved of their money or their corn.

shadow at Delphi : i.e. the empty privilege (as Demosthenes here chooses to represent it) of membership of the Amphictyonic League and Council, now claimed by Philip.

THE SECOND PHILIPPIC

§ 1. *sympathetic* : i.e. towards other Greek states, desirous of securing independence.

§ 11. *Alexander,* &c. Alexander of Macedon was sent by Mardonius, the Persian commander, to offer Athens alliance with Persia on favourable terms. Demosthenes has confused the order of events, and speaks as if this message was brought before the battle ⟨of Sal⟩amis. The Athenians left the city twice, before the bat⟨tle of S⟩alamis and before that of Plataeae; it was after Salamis ⟨that Al⟩exander was sent (Herod. viii. 140, &c.).

§ 14. ⟨at⟩ *Elateia*. This would be a menace to Thebes (cf. Speech ⟨on th⟩e Crown, §§ 174, 175). Elateia commands the road from ⟨Thermop⟩ylae to Thebes.

§ 19. *w⟨ell-minde⟩d* (σωφρονοῦσι), or 'free from passion', i.e. not liable ⟨to be carr⟩ied away by ambition or cupidity as th⟨e⟩ Thebans wer⟨e. It is⟩ different from mere 'good sense' (εὖ φρονεῖ, νοῦν ἔχει). ⟨For The⟩ban 'stupidity', see Speech on Peac⟨e⟩ § 15 (and n.).

§ 22. *Coun⟨cils of⟩ Ten* (δεκαδαρχίαν). It is clear that some so⟨rt⟩ of oligarchical ⟨govern⟩ment, nominated by Philip, is referred t⟨o⟩ but the relation ⟨of the⟩se to the tetrarchies mentioned in the Speec⟨h⟩ on the Chersone⟨se, § 3⟩6, as established by Philip, is uncertain. These correspond⟨ed to⟩ the four tribes or divisions of Thessaly (Thessaliotis, Phthi⟨otis,⟩ Pelasgiotis, Histiaeotis); and this is confirmed by a statement in Theopompus' forty-fourth book, to which Harpocration (s. v. δεκαδαρχία) refers. Harpocration states that Philip did not establish a decadarchy in Thessaly; and if he is right, then either (*a*) Demosthenes purposely used an inaccurate word, in order to suggest to the Messenians the idea of a government like that of the Councils of Ten established some sixty years before by Sparta in the towns subject to her; or (*b*) the text is wrong, and δεκαδαρχίαν is a misreading of Δ̄ΑΡΧΙΑΝ, in which Δ was the numeral (=4), and the whole stood for τετραρχίαν. As to (*a*), it is difficult to suppose that the Messenians would not know what had happened in Thessaly so well that the innuendo would fall flat. There is no evidence that 'decadarchy' could be used simply as a synonym for 'oligarchy'. As to (*b*), the supposed corruption is possible; but then we are left with τετραρχίαν where we should expect τετραρχίας: for there is no parallel to τετραρχία (sing.) in the sense of 'a system of tetrarchies'. It is, however, quite possible that Demosthenes was thinking especially of the Thessalians of Pherae, and of the particular tetrarchy established over them : and this seems on the whole the best solution. If, on the other hand, Harpocration is wrong, the reference here may be to a Council of Ten, either established previously to the tetrarchies, and superseded by them, or else coexistent with and superior to them ; in either case, since the singular is used, this decadarchy must have been a single government over the whole of Thessaly (or perhaps of the district about Pherae only), not a number of Councils, one in each city or division of Thessaly. (Theopompus' forty-fourth book probably dealt with 342 B. C., two years after the present speech, though before the Speech on the Chersonese ; but we are not told that he assigned the establishment of the tetrarchies to that year.)

§ 25. *find yourselves slaves* : lit. ' find your master.'

§ 28. *by yourselves* : i. e. in the absence of the ambassadors from Philip and other States.

who conveyed the promises : i. e. Ctesiphon, Aristodemus, and Neoptolemus (see Speech on Embassy, §§ 12, 94, 315, &c.) : but Demosthenes has probably Aeschines also in view.

§ 30. *water-drinker*. See Speech on Embassy, § 46.

§ 32. *secure myself as good a hearing*. Most editions accept this rendering of ἐμαυτῷ λόγον ποιήσω. But though λόγον διδόναι =' grant a hearing,' and λόγου τυχεῖν=' get a hearing,' λόγον ἑαυτῷ ποιεῖν is strange for ' secure oneself a hearing ', and the passage regularly quoted from the Speech against Aristocrates, § 81, is not parallel, since τούτῳ in that passage is not a reflexive pronoun, and λόγον πεποίηκε almost=λόγον δέδωκε. Possibly the text is corrupt, and we should either read ψόγον (with H. Richards) or ἐμαυτοῦ (' make you take as much account of me as of my opponents ').

further claim : since an attack on the part of Demosthenes would incite them to make out a plausible case for Philip once more, and so earn his gratitude.

ON THE EMBASSY

[The li   l translation of the title is 'On the misconduct as ambassad

§ 1.   *dra   your lots.*   The jurors who were to serve in each trial were se   d by lot out of the total number of jurors for the year.

§ 2.   *one of,   :* i. e. Timarchus (see Introd.).

   supremacy   e sovereignty of the people was exercised to a great extent tʁᵗ   the law-courts, the jury being always large enough to be fai   presentative of popular opinion, though probably there wasʰ   ally a rather disproportionate preponderance of poorer men among the jurors, the payment being insufficient to attract others. (See Introduction, vol. i, pp. 18, 19, 23.)

§ 11.   *the Ten Thousand :* the General Assembly of the Arcadians at Megalopolis.

§ 13.   *he came to me,* &c. Aeschines denies this, saying that it would have been absurd, when he knew that Demosthenes and Philocrates had acted together throughout (see Introd.).

§ 16.   *in the very presence,* &c. : contrast Speech on the Crown, § 23 (and see n. there). Aeschines states that he was in fact replying to inflammatory speeches made by orators who pointed to the Propylaea, and appealed to the memory of ancestral exploits ; and that he simply urged that it was possible for the Athenians to copy the wisdom of their forefathers without giving way to an unseasonable passion for strife.

§ 17.   *had again acted :* i. e. as on the First Embassy, if the reading is correct (or perhaps, 'had committed a fresh series of wrongful acts '). But possibly πεπρακότων is right, 'had sold fresh concessions ' to Philip.

§ 20.   Aeschines replies that every one expected Philip to turn against Thebes ; and that for the rest, he was only reporting the gossip of the Macedonian camp, where the representatives of many states were gathered together, and not making promises at all. It is noteworthy, however, that in the Speech on the Peace,

§ 10, shortly after the events in question, when the speeches made would be fresh in every one's memory, Demosthenes gives the same account of his opponent's assertions; and Aeschines probably said something very like what is attributed to him.

§ 21. *debt due to the god* : i.e. the value of the Temple-treasure of Delphi, which the Phocians had plundered.

§ 30. *for however contemptible*, &c. The argument seems to be this. ' You must not say that a man like Aeschines could not have brought about such vast results. Athens may employ inferior men, but any one who represents Athens has to deal with great affairs, and so his acts may have great consequences. And again, although it may have been Philip who actually ruined the Phocians, and although Aeschines could never have done it alone, still he did his best to help.'

§ 31. *the Town Hall*, or Prytaneum, where the Prytanes (the acting Committee of the Council) met, and other magistrates had their offices.

Timagoras was accused (according to Xenophon) by his colleague Leon of having conspired with Pelopidas of Thebes against the interests of Athens, when on a mission to the court of Artaxerxes in 357. In § 137 Demosthenes also states that he received large sums of money from Artaxerxes.

§ 36. Aeschines denies that he wrote the letter for Philip, and his denial is fairly convincing.

§ 40. *a talent*. According to Aristotle (*Eth. Nic.* v. 7) the conventional amount payable as ransom was one mina per head. But from § 169 it appears that the Macedonians sometimes asked for more than this.

laudable ambition : i.e. to get credit for having thought of the ransom of the prisoners.

§ 47. *handed in* : either to the Clerk or to the Proedroi (the committee of Chairmen of the Assembly).

§ 51. Aeschines states that Philip's invitation was declined because it was suggested that Philip would keep the soldiers sent as hostages.

§ 65. *on our way to Delphi*. Demosthenes had been one of the Athenian representatives at the meeting of the Amphictyonic Council at Delphi this year.

gave its vote, &c. After the battle of Aegospotami at the end of the Peloponnesian War, the representative of Thebes proposed to the Spartans and their allies that Athens should be destroyed and its inhabitants sold into slavery.

§ 70. *read this law over* : i. e. that the herald might proclaim it after him.

§ 72. For the Spartans see § 76. The Phocians had treated the Athenians badly when Proxenus was sent to Thermopylae (see Introd. to Speech on Peace). Hegesippus may have opposed the acceptance of Philip's invitation to the Athenians to join him. Aeschines (on the Embassy, §§ 137, 138) mentions no names in connexion with the refusal, but represents it as the sacrifice of a unique opportunity of saving the Phocians (cf. § 51 n.).

§ 76. *deceit and cunning, and of nothing else* (πᾶσα ἀπάτη). The argument is, ' Aeschines will try to allege wrongful acts on the part of the Phocians ; but there was no time for such acts in the five days ; and this proves that there were no such acts to justify their ruin, and that their overthrow was due to nothing but trickery.' This is better than to translate ' *every kind of* deceit and trickery was concocted for the ruin of the Phocians ' ; for this is not the point, nor is it what would be inferred from the fact that there was only a five-days' interval between the speech of Aeschines and the capitulation of the Phocians. There is no need to emend to ἡ πᾶσα ἀπάτη.

on account of the Peace : i. e. of the negotiations for the Peace, before it was finally arranged.

all that they wished : viz. the restoration of the Temple of Delphi to their kinsmen, the Dorians of Mount Parnassus.

§ 78. *four whole months* : in reality, three months and a few days.

§ 81. *Phocian people* : i. e. those who were left in Phocis, as distinct from the exiles just referred to.

§ 86. *of Diophantus.* In 352, when Philip had been repulsed by Onomarchus, Diophantus proposed that public thanksgivings should be held (see Introd. to First Philippic).

of Callisthenes : in 346, after the Phocians had surrendered to Philip.

the sacrifice to Heracles : perhaps one of the two festivals which were respectively held at Marathon and at Cynosarges.

§ 99. *constitutional* : lit. ' an excuse for a citizen,' under a constitution by which no one was compelled to enter public life, and any one who did so without the requisite capacity had to take the responsibility for his errors.

§ 103. *impeached.* An impeachment was brought before the Council (or, more rarely, the Assembly). The procedure was only applied to cases of extraordinary gravity, and particularly to what would now be called cases of treason.

§ 114. *by torture.* The evidence of slaves might be given under torture, in response to a challenge from one or other of the parties to a suit. The most diverse opinions as to the value of such evidence are expressed by the orators, according to the requirements of their case. The consent of both sides was necessary; and in a very large number of cases, one side or the other appears to have refused to allow evidence to be taken in this way.

was going : i. e. to Philip.

§ 118. *accept his discharge.* There seems to be a play on two senses of the verb ἀφιέναι, viz. ' to discharge from the obligations of a contract ', and ' to acquit '.

§ 120. *Why, this is the finest,* &c. The expression (τοῦτο γάρ ἐστι τὸ λαμπρόν) recurs in § 279, a closely parallel passage, and need not be regarded as an interpolation in either case. The interpretation given seems slightly preferable, and is approved by Weil. It is almost equally possible to translate the Greek by ' such is the brilliant defence which he offers '; but perhaps this does not suit § 279 so well.

stand up. Apparently Aeschines declined the invitation,

which was quite within the custom of the Athenian courts. Either of the principal parties could ask the other questions, and have the answers taken down as evidence.

cases that have all, &c. The reference is to the prosecution of Timarchus, when advanced in age, for offences committed in early youth. There may also be an allusion to Aeschines' early career as an actor.

§ 122. *declined on oath.* An elected official could refuse to serve, if he took an oath that there was some good reason (such as illness) for excusing him.

§ 126. *though not elected.* Aeschines (on the Embassy, § 94) replies that in fact the commission was renewed at a second meeting of the Assembly, and that he was then well enough to go and was elected. (That there was a second election of ambassadors is confirmed by Demosthenes' own statement in § 172 of the present speech, that he himself was twice elected and twice refused to serve.)

§ 128. *Thesmothetae*: the six archons who did not hold the special offices of archon eponymus, polemarch, or king archon.

Aeschines went, &c. To have refused to be present would really have been to make a political demonstration against Thebes, which would have had perilous results. Aeschines defends himself on the ground that in his view the Peace was no disadvantage to Athens, so that he might well join in the honours paid to the Gods.

§ 129. *Metroon.* The temple of the Great Mother (Cybele), which was the Athenian record-office.

the name of Aeschines: i.e. its removal from the list of ambassadors.

§ 131. *in their interest.* If the words are not corrupt, the meaning is probably ' in the interest of Philip and the Thebans '; or possibly, ' in reference to these matters.'

§ 136. *as his informant.* The text is possibly corrupt, though as it stands it might perhaps bear the meaning given, if ὑπάρχει were understood with αὐτίς. Others (with or without emendation) take the sense to be 'to manage his business . . . just as he would manage it in person'.

§ 137. For Timagoras see § 31 n.

§ 144. *summon Philip's envoys* : i. e. in order to report the decision of the Assembly, and so close the matter.

§ 147. *ask him whether*, &c. The argument seems to be this ' if Aeschines was the ambassador of a city which had been victorious against Philip, the latter would naturally wish to buy [e]asy terms of peace ; and Aeschines might undertake to procure [s]uch terms, without committing a particularly heinous offence, [si]nce he would only be getting some advantage for himself out of [t]he general good fortune of his country. But to secure advantages for himself at his country's expense, when his country was already suffering disaster, would be far worse. And as Aeschines complains that the generals *had* incurred disaster, he convicts himself of the worse offence.'

§ 148. The *Tilphossaeum* was apparently a mountain near Lake Copais in Boeotia. The town which Strabo calls Tilphusium may have been on the mountain. Neones, or Neon, was a Phocian village ; Hedyleion, a mountain in Boeotia.

§ 149. *Ah ! he will say*, &c. Either the words are interpolated, or there is a lacuna. The objection is nowhere refuted.

§ 156. *Doriscus*, &c. The places mentioned did not really belong to Athens, but to Cersobleptes, who was being assisted by Athenian troops, so that, strictly speaking, Philip was within his rights ; and in fact (according to Aeschines), Cersobleptes and the Sacred Mountain were taken by Philip the day before the Athenians and their allies swore to the Peace at Athens.

§ 162. *Eucleides* had been sent to protest against Philip's attack upon Cersobleptes in 346 (see vol. i, p. 122). Philip replied that he had not yet been officially informed by the Athenian ambassadors of the conclusion of the Peace, and was therefore not yet bound by it.

§ 166. *procure their ransom* : i. e. from the various Macedonians who had captured them, or to whom they had been given or sold.

§ 176. *committed to writing*, &c. Formal evidence (as distinct from the mere assertions of a speaker) was written down, and the witness was asked to swear to it. A witness who was called upon might swear that he had no knowledge of the matter in question (ἐξόμνυσθαι). By writing down his evidence and swearing to it, Demosthenes took the risk of prosecution for perjury.

§ 180. *might be proved in countless ways* : or 'would need : speech of infinite length'. But as καί and not δέ follows, I slightl' prefer the former rendering. (The latter is supported by th' Third Philippic, § 60, but there the next clause is connected by δέ

Ergophilus was heavily fined in 362 (see Speech again: Aristocrates, § 104); Cephisodotus in 358 (ibid. § 167, an: Aeschines against Ctesiphon, § 52); Timomachus went into exile in 360 to escape condemnation (against Aristocrates, § 115, &c.). Ergocles was perhaps the friend of Thrasybulus (see Lysias, Orations xxviii, xxix), and may have been condemned for his conduct in Thrace, as well as for malversation at Halicarnassus. Dionysius is unknown.

§ 187. *has got beyond*, &c. : an ironical way of saying that he has so much overdone his application to himself of the title of (prospective) 'benefactor' of Athens, that another word (e.g. 'deceiver') would be more appropriate. The word ψυχρόν is (at least by Greek literary critics) applied to strong expressions out of place, and here also, probably, of an exaggerated phrase which falls flat. This is perhaps the best interpretation of a very difficult passage.

§ 191. For Timagoras, see § 31 n. Tharrex and Smicythus are unknown. Adeimantus was one of the generals at Aegospotami, the only Athenian prisoner spared by Lysander, and on that account suspected of treason by the Athenians, and prosecuted by Conon (called 'the elder', to distinguish him from his grandson, who was a contemporary of Demosthenes).

§ 194. *guest-friend*. The term (ξένος) was applied to the relationship (more formal than that of simple friendship) between citizens of different states, who were bound together by ties of hospitality and mutual goodwill.

§ 19..   ..*irty* : i.e. the 'Thirty Tyrants' who ruled Athens
..   ..ort of Sparta) for a few months in 403.   See n. on

..   Aeschines warmly denies this story. He says that
Demosthenes tried to bribe Aristophanes of Olynthus to swear
that it was true, and that the woman was his own wife. He adds
that the jury, on an appeal from Eubulus, refused to let Demosthenes complete the story.

§ 199.   *initiations* : see Speech on Crown, §§ 259 ff., with notes.

§ 200.   *played the rogue.* The scholiast says that clerks were
sometimes bribed to alter the laws and decrees which they read
to the Court ; and a magistrates' clerk had doubtless plenty of
opportunities for conniving at petty frauds.

§ 204.   *should not have been sworn to.* This is out of chrono-
logical order as it stands, and emendations have been proposed,
but unnecessarily.

§ 209.   *would not have him for your representative* : in the
question about Athenian rights at Delos. See Introduction to
the Speech.

§ 213.   *I have no further time*, &c. : lit. ' no one will pour water
for me ' into the water-clock, by which all trials were regulated.

§ 221.   *consider*, &c. There is an anacoluthon in the Greek,
which may be literally translated, ' Consider, if, where I who am
absolutely guiltless was afraid of being ruined by them—what
ought these men themselves, the actual criminals, to suffer ? '

§ 222.   *get money out of you* : i.e. to be bought off.

§ 230.   *choregus and trierarch* : see Introd. to Speech on Naval
Boards, and n. on Philippic I. § 36.

§ 231.   *all was well* (εὐθενεῖσθαι). The reading is almost
certainly wrong. Weil rightly demands some word contrasting
with ἀγνοεῖν (' did not understand his country ') in the corre-
sponding clause.

§ 237.   *vase-cases* : i.e. boxes to contain bottles of oil or per-
fume for toilet use.

§ 245.   *the cock-pit.* That this is the meaning seems to be
proved by the words of Aeschines (against Timarchus, § 53) ;

otherwise the natural translation would be ' to the bird-market '.
Cocks were no doubt sold in the bird-market; but Aeschines
refers directly to cock-fighting, not to the purchase of the birds.

§ 246. *hack-writers* : lit. ' speech-writers,' who composed
speeches for litigants, and no doubt padded them out with
quotations from poets, as well as with rhetorical commonplaces.
Demosthenes taunts Aeschines particularly with ransacking
unfamiliar plays, instead of those he knew well.

§ 249. *reared up . . . greatness* : or possibly, ' reared up al
these sons of hers.'

Hero-Physician. See Speech on the Crown, § 129 n.

Round Chamber, in the Prytaneum or Town Hall (see § 31 n.

§ 252. *at the risk of his own life.* He tried to avoid the ris
by feigning madness. Salamis was in the hands of the Megarean
and the Athenians had become so weary of their unsuccessfu
attempts to recover it, that they decreed the penalty of death
upon any one who proposed to make a fresh attempt. The verses,
however, which are quoted in the text, are probably derived not
from the poem which Solon composed for this purpose, but from
another of his political poems.

§ 255. *with a cap on your head.* Plutarch (Solon 82 c) says
that ' Solon burst into the market-place suddenly, with a cap on
his head '. The cap was intended to suggest that he had just
returned from Salamis, since it was the custom to wear a cap only
when on a journey, or in case of illness (cf. Plato, *Republic*, iii.
406 *d*). There may possibly be an allusion also to Aeschines' own
alleged sickness (§ 136 above), but this is very doubtful. The
words more probably mean, ' however closely you copy Solon '
(as you copied his attitude in speaking), ' when you run about
declaiming against me.'

§ 257. *accepted the challenge.* At the examination before the
Board of Auditors (Logistae) the question was almost certainly
put, whether any one present wished to challenge the report of
the ambassador under examination.

§ 259. *claim* (ἀξιούμενοι) : or, ' are thought worthy ' ; but the first sense is much better in the parallel passage in § 295, and this ' middle ' use seems to be sufficiently attested, though the active voice is used in the same sense in § 338.

§ 260. *paramount position* : i.e. among the tribes of North Greece (Magnetes, Perrhaebi, &c.).

§ 264. *concluded the war*, &c. In 383 B.C. In fact, however, they only obtained peace by joining the Spartan alliance.

§ 271. *Arthmius* : see Philippic III. § 42 (and note).

§ 273. *Callias*, in 444 B.C. Cf. Speech for the Rhodians, § 29. The Chelidonian Islands lay off the south coast of Lycia, the Cyanean rocks at the northern mouth of the Bosporus.

§ 277. *Epicrates* was sent as ambassador to Persia early in the fourth century, and received large presents. According to Plutarch he escaped condemnation ; but he may have been tried more than once. The comic poets make fun of his long beard.

who brought the people back from the Peiraeus. Thrasybulus occupied the Peiraeus in 403, secured the expulsion of the Thirty Tyrants from Athens, and restored the democracy.

§ 278. *the decree* : i.e. the decree by which Epicrates and his colleagues were condemned.

§ 279. *for this is the splendid thing* : cf. § 120 n.

§ 280. *exiled* and *punished*. We should perhaps (with Weil) read *ἤ* (' or ') for *καί* (' and ').

descendant of Harmodius : i.e. Proxenus, who had been only recently condemned, and is therefore not named.

§ 281. *another priestess*. According to the scholiast, the reference is to Ninus, a priestess of Sabazios, who was prosecuted by Menecles for making love-potions for young men. The connexion of this offence with the meetings of the initiated is left to be understood.

§ 282. *the burden undertaken*. Such burdens as the duties of choregus, trierarch, &c., might be voluntarily undertaken, as they were by Demosthenes (see n. on Philippic I. § 36).

§ 287. *Cyrebion*, or ' Light-as-Chaff ', was the nickname of Epicrates, Aeschines' brother-in-law (not the Epicrates of § 277).

as a reveller, no doubt in some Dionysiac revel, in which it was not considered decent to take part without a mask. (The original purpose of masks, however, was not to conceal one's identity from motives of shame, though Demosthenes suggests it as a motive here.)

were water flowing upstream. A half-proverbial expression implying that the world was being turned upside-down, when such a person could prosecute for such offences.

§ 290. *Hegesilaus* was one of the generals sent to Euboea to help Plutarchus ; cf. Speech on the Peace, § 5 n. He was accused of abetting Plutarchus in the deception which he practised upon Athens. For Thrasybulus, cf. § 277.

the primary question : i. e. of the guilt or innocence of the defendant. If he was pronounced guilty, the question of sentence (or damages) had to be argued and decided separately.

§ 295. *claim to be* : cf. n. on § 259.

churning the butter (ἐτύρευε) : i. e. concocting the plot. (For the metaphor cf. Aristophanes, *Knights* 479.)

§ 299. *Zeus and Dione.* These names show that the oracles referred to were probably given at Dodona.

§ 303. *oath of the young soldiers.* When the young Athenian came of age, he received a shield and spear in the temple of Aglaurus, and swore to defend his country and to uphold its constitution (cf. Lycurgus, *Against Leocrates*, § 76).

§ 314. *keeping step with Pythocles*, who was a tall man, while Aeschines was short.

§ 326. *Drymus and Panactum* were on the border between Boeotia and Attica. Nothing else is known of the expedition.

§ 332. *Chares.* See nn. on Philippic I. §§ 24, 46 ; Olynthiac II. § 28, and Introductions.

§ 333. *of one of whom*, &c. : i. e. of Philip (see § 111 ff., and Introd. to Speech on the Peace).

§ 342. *Euthycrates.* See Introd. to Olynthiacs.

ON THE CHERSONESE

§ 9. The argument is, 'if Philip is not committing hostilities so long as he keeps away from Attica, Diopeithes is not doing so, so long as he keeps away from Macedonia, and only operates in Thrace.'

drive the vessels, &c. See Speech on the Peace, § 25 n.

§ 14. *passing the time*: i.e. until a convenient season for an attack arrives.

those who are on the spot: i.e. in Thrace, and who had doubtless sent messages to Athens. Others think that the words mean 'those who are here from Thrace'.

Etesian winds. See First Philippic, § 31 n.

infatuation: i.e. hostility to Athens.

§ 16. *punish the settlers* : those who were sent with Diopeithes and demanded admission to Cardia.

§ 18. *Chalcis*, in Euboea (see Introd.).

§ 21. *keep our hands*, &c., *sea uses*: a reference to the distributions of Festival-Money (see Third Olynthiac, with Introduction and notes).

contributions of the allies. This interpretation seems on the whole better warranted than 'contributions promised to Diopeithes'.

§ 24. *I consent to any penalty*, &c. 'I assess my own penalty at anything'—a metaphor from the practice of the law-courts, which allowed a convicted prisoner to practise an alternative penalty to that suggested by the prosecutor.

Erythraeans: Erythrae was on the coast of Asia Minor, opposite Chios.

§ 25. *benevolences*: the same word as was used of the forced contributions levied by English kings.

§ 27. *surrendering*: i.e. to his soldiers, to be plundered (if the phrase is meant to convey anything but a vague accusation).

§ 28. *wax-tablet*: i.e. a summons.

M 2

so many ships. The critics of Diopeithes must have proposed the sending of a definite force to control him.

§ 29. *a dispatch-boat* : lit. ' the *Paralus* '. This ship, and the *Salaminia*, were the two vessels regularly employed on public errands.

spitefulness : i.e. towards Diopeithes.

§ 30. *Chares* : see references in n. on Speech on Embassy, § 332.

Aristophon. The reference may be to his conduct as general in the early days of the war with Philip about Amphipolis. His activity as a statesman began as far back as 403, and he was one of the most influential politicians in Athens from about 361 to 354.

§ 31. *losing something* : *sc.* a scapegoat whom you could punish.

§ 40. *Euthycrates*, &c. See Introd. to Olynthiacs.

§ 44. *wretched hamlets* (κακῶν): lit. ' evils ' or ' miseries ' ; but the word is possibly corrupt. (The original reading may possibly have been καλυβῶν.) According to the scholiast, Drongilum and Cabyle are near Amphipolis and the Strymon ; but others assign different localities to them. Masteira is quite unknown.

§ 45. *pit of destruction* (βαράθρῳ). This was literally the pit into which the bodies of condemned criminals were thrown at Athens.

silos : underground store-houses for grain, such as were found in Ceos not many years ago, and may still be in use.

§ 46. *irremediable* (ἀνήκεστον). The reading of two good manuscripts ἀνείκαστον (otherwise only known as a late Greek word) may be correct. If so, it may mean ' unparalleled ', or ' inexplicable '.

§ 57. The meaning is, that by denouncing those who propose active measures now, they are preparing the way in order to prosecute them so soon as you find the war burdensome ; whereas they should themselves be prosecuted for letting things go as far as they have gone.

§ 59. *Oreus.* See Introd.

Pheraeans, in 344. See Introd. to Second Philippic ; and cf. Third Philippic, § 12.

compromise. Slavery seems to be ironically regarded as a compromise between activity and quiescence.

§ 63. *robbed of at an earlier period.* The sense must either be this, or else ' all that you have lost in open war '. In either case emendation is required.

§ 70. *trierarch and choregus.* Demosthenes was choregus in 348, and trierarch in 363, 359, and 357.

§ 74. *Timotheus* : in 358, when Athens liberated Euboea from the Thebans. Cf. First Philippic, § 17, First Olynthiac, § 8. The effect of Timotheus' speech was such that the expedition started within three days. (Speech against Androtion, § 14.)

§ 75. *best counsel that he can.* The text is probably corrupt ; but this was probably the sense of the original.

THE THIRD PHILIPPIC

§ 2. *actively at work* : the reference is to Diopeithes (see Speech on Chersonese, § 57).

§§ 4, 5. Passages are repeated from the Speech on the Chersonese, § 4, and First Philippic, § 2.

§ 8. *not to defraud us* : i. e. by making statements which he is not prepared to act upon.

§ 11. *as though visiting his allies.* This is not true, though envoys from the Phocians, as from most other Greek states of importance, were in Philip's camp. With the whole passage, cf. Speech on Embassy, §§ 20 ff.

§ 12. *Pherae.* See Speech on Chersonese, § 59 n. For Oreus see Introd. to Speech on Chersonese, and §§ 33 and 59 ff. of this Speech.

§ 15. *Serrhium*, &c. See Introd. to Speech on Peace.

he had sworn to a Peace. This is untrue ; see Speech on Embassy, § 156, where it is part of the charge against Aeschines' party, that they had enabled Philip to take these places *before* he had sworn to the Peace.

§ 16. *religion* : with special reference here to the sanctity of the oath.

into the Chersonese : i. e. to help Cardia. The claim of Athens to Cardia was not good, and it appears from the Speech of Hegesippus against Halonnesus, § 42, that the Athenians had recognized the independence of the town.

§ 18. *if anything should happen* : e. g. the outbreak of open war, or (more probably) a defeat.

§ 23. *seventy-three years* : i. e. 476–404 B. C.

thirty years save one : i. e. 404–376 B. C. (in the latter year Chabrias defeated the Spartans off Naxos).

battle of Leuctra : in 371 B. C.

§ 24. *disturb the established order* : i. e. by establishing garchical governments in place of democracy.

§ 26. *in the Thracian region* : strictly, in Chalcidice and the neighbourhood. See Introd. to Olynthiacs.

robbed their very cities of their governments. This is preferable to the (grammatically) equally possible rendering, ' robbed them of their constitutions and their cities,' as it suits the facts better. Philip seems to have substituted tetrarchies for separate city-states. (See Speech on Chersonese, § 26, and Second Philippic, § 22 n.)

§ 27. *Ambracia.* See Introd. to Speech on Chersonese. *Elis*: Introd. to Speech on Embassy. *Megara* : Speech on Embassy, §§ 294, 295.

§ 32. *Pythian games.* See Introd. to Speech on Peace. In 342 Philip sent a deputy to preside in his name.

§§ 33, 34. See Introd. to Speech on Chersonese. Echinus was a Theban colony in Thessaly, on the north coast of the Malian Gulf.

§ 42. *Arthmius*, &c. (cf. Speech on Embassy, § 271). Zeleia was in the Troad, near Cyzicus. Arthmius was apparently proxenus of Athens at Zeleia, and as such had probably certain rights at Athens, of which the decree deprived him ; so that Demosthenes' remarks at the beginning of § 44 are slightly misleading.

§ 46. At the end of this section two versions are imperfectly blended, and it does not appear what were the contents of the document. Some suppose that the insertion 'He reads from the document' is an early conjectural interpolation.

§ 49. *because he leads*, &c. Philip did, in fact, bring the Macedonian heavy infantry to great perfection for the purposes of a pitched battle, though the decisive action was generally that of the cavalry. But the other troops which Demosthenes names would enable him to execute rapid movements with success. The use of light-armed troops had already been developed by the Athenian general, Iphicrates.

§ 50. *with such advantages* : lit. 'under these conditions' (*not* ' to crown all ', nor ' at the head of these troops ').

§ 52. Contrast Speech on Naval Boards, § 9.

§§ 57 ff. See Introd. to Speech on Embassy.

§ 59. Euphraeus had been a disciple of Plato, and an adviser of Perdiccas, Philip's elder brother. It was he who recommended Perdiccas to entrust the government of part of Macedonia to Philip, whom he afterwards so strongly opposed.

§ 72. *embassies.* See Introd. to Speech on Chersonese.

ON THE CROWN

§ 1. *to take counsel*, &c. Aeschines had asked the jury to refuse Demosthenes a hearing, or at least to require him to follow the same order of treatment as himself.

§ 3. *unpleasant.* Many render δυσχερές 'inauspicious', 'ill-omened' ; but as we do not know exactly what was in Demosthenes' mind, it is better not to give the word a meaning which it does not bear elsewhere. It may, however, mean 'vexatious'.

§ 11. *knave as you are*, &c. The assonance of the original might perhaps be partly reproduced by rendering ' evil-minded as you are, it was yet a very simple-minded idea that your mind conceived ', &c.

§ 12. *it does not enable the State* : lit. ' it is not possible for the State.' The point is that the prosecution of Ctesiphon, while expressing the malice of Aeschines towards Demosthenes, does not enable the State to punish Demosthenes himself for his alleged offences, since any penalty inflicted would fall on Ctesiphon.

§ 13. *to debar another*, &c. This probably refers to the attempt to deprive Demosthenes of a hearing, not (as some have thought) to the attempt to get so heavy a fine inflicted upon Ctesiphon that he would be unable to pay it, and would therefore lose his rights as a citizen.

§ 17. *ascribed to me*, &c. Aeschines was anxious, in view of the existing state of feeling at Athens, to disown his part in connexion with the Peace of Philocrates; while Demosthenes undoubtedly assisted Philocrates in the earlier of the negotiations and discussions which led to the Peace.

appropriate. ' The recapitulation of the history is not a mere argumentative necessity, but has a moral fitness also; in fact, the whole defence of Demosthenes resolves itself into a proof that he only acted in the spirit of Athenian history ' (Simcox).

§ 18. *When the Phocian war had broken out*: i.e. in 356-5. Demosthenes made his first speech in the Assembly in 354.

those who detested the Spartans: i.e. the Messenians and Arcadians.

those who had previously governed, &c.: e.g. the oligarchies which had governed with the help of Sparta in Phlius and Mantinea, and were overthrown after the battle of Leuctra.

§ 19. *would be forced*, &c. This is a misrepresentation, since Philip and the Thebans had been in alliance for some time, and Thebes had no such grounds for apprehending evil from Philip, as would make her apply to Athens.

§ 21. *Aristodemus*, &c. See Introd. to Speech on the Peace. As a matter of fact, Demosthenes acted with Philocrates at least down to the return of the First Embassy, and himself proposed to crown Aristodemus for his services (Aeschines, On the Embassy, §§ 15–17).

§ 23. *the Hellenes had all*, &c. It is not easy to reconcile this passage with § 16 of the Speech on the Embassy, from which it appears that representatives of other states were present in Athens; but these so-called envoys may have been private visitors, and in any case there was no real hope of uniting Greece against Philip.

§ 24. *Eurybatus* is said to have been sent as an envoy by Croesus to Cyrus, and to have turned traitor. The name came to be proverbial.

§ 27. *those strongholds.* See Introd. to Speech on the Peace.

§ 28. *But they would have watched*, &c. The passage has been taken in several ways: (1) ' They would have had to watch,' &c., and this would have been discreditable to Athens; (2) ' They would have watched,' &c., i. e. they would not have been excluded, as you desired, in any case; (3) ' But, you say, they would have paid two obols apiece,' and the city would have gained this. The sentence which follows favours (3), but perhaps (2) is best. The petty interests of the city would include (from the point of view assumed by Aeschines) the abstention from showing civility to the enemy's envoys. The two-obol (threepenny) seats were the cheapest.

§ 30. *three whole months.* In fact the ambassadors were only absent from Athens about ten weeks altogether.

equally well. The reading (ὁμοίως) is probably wrong; but if it is right, this must be the meaning.

§ 32. *as you did before*, in 352. See Introd. to First Philippic.

§ 36. *decree of Callisthenes.* This ordered the bringing in of effects from the country. See Speech on Embassy, §§ 86, 125.

§ 41. *property in Boeotia.* See Speech on Embassy, § 145.

§ 43. *their hopes*: *sc.* of the humiliation of Thebes.

and gladly: i. e. they were glad to be free from a danger which (though remotely) threatened themselves, as the next sentence explains. I can see no good reason for taking the participle πολεμούμενοι as concessive (' *although* they also,' &c.).

§ 48. For *Lasthenes* see Introd. to Olynthiacs. Timolaus probably contrived the surrender of Thebes after the battle of Chaeroneia. Eudicus is unknown. Simus invoked Philip's aid

against the ty͏r͏ s at Pherae in 352 (see Introd. to First Philippic).
Aristratus w e   rant of Sicyon, and made alliance with Philip in
338. For h͏as   s, see Speech on Embassy, § 295.

§ 50. s th   regs : strictly the remains, and especially the
wine left he   e cups, from the previous night's feast ; here
the long ad   ed responsibility of Aeschines for the Peace
of 346. ey

§ 63. es.   es : a small tribe living to the south-west of
Thessaly

§ 65 who   onstitutions. This refers especially to the Thessalians, ably   l been placed under tetrarchies (see Philippic III.
§ 26). le to

§ 7 ould   tophon. See Speech on Chersonese, § 30 n. Dio-
peith   haps Diopeithes of Sphettus (mentioned by Hype-
reide law   against Euxenippus, § 39), not the general sent by
Athe̊l on   e Chersonese.

§ ,   the events mentioned in this section, see Introd. to
Speech en   he Embassy.

§ 72.   ysian booty. A proverbial expression derived from
the helpless condition of Mysia (according to legend) in the absence
of its king, Telephus.

§ 79. to the Peloponnese, in 344 (see Introd. to Second Philippic):
to Euboea in 343–2 (see Introd. to Speech on Embassy) ; to Oreus,
&c., in 341 (see Introd. to this Speech).

§ 82. as their patron, i. e. as consul (or official patron) of Oreus
in Athens. See n. on Speech for Rhodians, § 15.

civil rights. See vol. i, p. 52.

§ 83. this was already the second proclamation : i. e. the proclamation in accordance with the decree of Aristonicus. It is indeed
just possible that the reference is to the proposal of Ctesiphon,
' for this is now the second proclamation,' &c. If so, we should
have to assume that the proclamation under the decree of
Demomeles in 338 was prevented by the disaster of Chaeroneia.
But the first sentence of § 120 is against this (see Goodwin's
edition ad loc.).

§ 94. *inconsiderate conduct*: i.e. in joining the revolt of the
thenian allies in 356.

§ 96. *when the Spartans*, &c. The section refers to the events
395.

Decelean War: i.e. the last part of the Peloponnesian War
3–404 B.C.), when Deceleia (in Attica) was occupied by the
rtans.

99. *Thebans . . . Euboea*: in 358 or 357. See Speech for
lopolitans, § 14 n.

100. *Oropus.* See Speech for Megalopolitans, § 11 n.

I was one. Demosthenes was, in fact, co-trierarch with
nus (Speech against Meidias, § 161).

02. See Speech on Naval Boards (with Introd. and notes),
1. on Olynthiac II, § 29.

btaining exemption. The undertaking of the trierarchy
:rred exemption from other burdens for the year, and (con-
ly) no one responsible for another public burden need be
arch. The leaders of the Taxation Boards referred to in
03 are probably not (as generally supposed) the richest men in
the *Naval* Boards [1] (responsible for trierarchy), but those in the
Hundred Boards responsible for the war tax. In each of these
Boards there was a leader, a 'second', and a 'third', and these, all
together, are almost certainly identical with the ' Three Hundred '
responsible for advancing the sum due. When these were
already advancing the war tax, they became exempt from
trierarchy, and their poorer colleagues in the Naval Boards (to
which of course they also belonged) had to bear the burden without them. But under Demosthenes' law the trierarchic payment
was required from all alike, in strict proportion to their valuation
as entered for the purposes of the war tax ; and the Three Hundred (the leaders, seconds, and thirds) were no longer exempted.
(This explains their anxiety to get the law shelved.) Even in

[1] They may indeed have been so, but it was in virtue of their
function as leading members of the Hundred Boards (for collecting
the war tax) that they were grouped together as the Three Hundred.

years when they were not exempt, before Demosthenes' law wa[s]
passed, they only paid a very small share in proportion to the[ir]
wealth, since all the members of each Naval Board paid the sam[e]
sum. It appears, however, that (though the Three Hundred [as]
such cannot be shown to have had any office in connexion wi[th]
the trierarchy) the richer men in the Naval Boards arranged [the]
contracts for the work of equipment, and that when they h[ad]
contracted that the work should be done (e. g.) for a talent, th[ey]
sometimes recovered the whole talent from their poorer colleagu[es]
(Speech against Meidias, § 155.)

§ 103. *lie under sworn notice*, &c. (ἐν ὑπωμοσίᾳ). One [who]
intended to indict the proposer of a law for illegality had prob[ably]
to give sworn notice of his intention, and the suggestion mad[e by]
Demosthenes was that when such notice had been given, he sh[ould]
let the law drop.

§ 105. *the decree*, &c. : i. e. either a decree suspending the [law]
until the indictment should be heard, or one ordering the tria[l of]
the indictment to be held.

§ 107. *no trierarch*, &c. A trierarch who thought the burd[en]
too heavy for him could appeal against it by laying a branch on
the altar in the Pnyx, or by taking sanctuary in the Temple of
Artemis at Munychia. A dilatory or recalcitrant trierarch could
be arrested by order of the ten commissioners (ἀποστολεῖς) who
constituted a sort of Admiralty Board.

§ 111. *the laws*, &c. The laws alleged to have been violated
were copied out, and accompanied the indictment. With regard
to the laws in the present case, see Goodwin's edition, pp. 313-6.

§ 114. *Nausicles* was sent to oppose Philip at Thermopylae in
352 (see Introd. to First Philippic). Diotimus had a command at
sea in 338, and his surrender was demanded by Alexander in 335,
as was also that of Charidemus (see n. on Olynthiac III, § 5), who
had now been a regular Athenian general for many years, and
had been sent to assist Byzantium in 340 (see Speech against
Aristocrates, *passim*).

§ 121. *hellebore* : supposed in antiquity to cure madness.

§ 122. *reveller on a cart*, e.g. on the second day of the Anthes-
teria, when masked revellers rode in wagons and assailed the
bystanders with abusive language. Such ceremonial abuse was
perhaps originally supposed to have power to avert evil, and
occurs in primitive ritual all over the world.

§ 125. *the statutable limit.* There was a limit of time (differing
according to the alleged offence) after which no action could be
brought. Demosthenes could not now be prosecuted for any of
the offences with which Aeschines charged him.

§ 127. *Aeacus*, &c. : the judges of the dead in Hades, according
to popular legend.

scandal-monger. The Greek word (σπερμολόγος) is used pri-
marily of a small bird that pecks up seeds, and hence of a person
who picks up petty gossip. (In Acts xvii. 18 it is the word which
is applied to St. Paul, and translated 'this babbler'.)

an old hand in the market-place : i.e. a rogue. A clerk
would perhaps often be found in the offices about the market-
place ; or the reference may be to the market-place as a centre
of gossip.

O Earth, &c. Demosthenes quotes from the peroration of
Aeschines' speech.

§ 129. The stories which Demosthenes retails in these sections
deal with a time which must have been forty or fifty years before
the date of this speech, and probably contain little truth, beyond
the facts that Aeschines' father was a schoolmaster (not a slave),
and was assisted by Aeschines himself ; and that his mother was
priestess of a ' thiasos ' or voluntary association of worshippers of
Dionysus-Sabazios, among whose ceremonies was doubtless one
symbolizing a marriage or mystical union between the god and
his worshippers. (Whether the form of ' sacred marriage ' which
was originally intended to promote the fertility of the ground by
' sympathetic magic ' entered into the ritual of Sabazios is doubtful.) Such a rite, though probably in fact quite innocent, gave rise
to suspicions, of which Demosthenes takes full advantage ; and the
fact that well-known courtesans (such as Phryne and perhaps

Ninus) sometimes organized such 'mysteries' would lend colour
to the suspicions.

Hero of the Lancet (τῷ καλαμίτῃ ἥρῳι). The interpretation is
very uncertain (see Goodwin, pp. 339 ff.); and, according as
κάλαμος is taken in the sense of 'lancet', 'splints', or 'bow',
editors render the phrase 'hero of the lancet', 'hero of the splints',
'archer-hero' (identified by some with Toxaris, the Scythian
physician, whose arrival in Athens in Solon's time is described in
Lucian's Σκύθης ἢ Πρόξενος). That the Hero was a physician is
shown by the Speech on the Embassy, § 249.

§ 130. *for they were not like*, &c. (οὐδὲ γὰρ ὧν ἔτυχεν ἦν, ἀλλ' οὓς
ὁ δῆμος καταρᾶται). The meaning is quite uncertain. The most
likely interpretations are : (1) that given in the text, ἃ βεβίω...
being understood as the subject of ἦν, and ὧν ἔτυχεν as = τούτων ἃ
ἔτυχεν, i. e. 'not belonging to the class of acts which were such as
chance made them,' but acts of a quite definite kind, viz. the kind
which the People curses (through the mouth of the herald at each
meeting of the Assembly); (2) 'for he was not of ordinary parents,
but of such as the People curses'; the subject of ἦν being
Aeschines. But there is the difficulty that, with this subject for
ἦν, ὧν ἔτυχέν can only represent τούτων ὧν ἔτυχεν ὤν, whereas
the sense required is τούτων οἳ ἔτυχον, or (the regular idiom) τῶν
τυχόντων; and the sense is not so good, for the context (ὄψε γάρ)
shows that the clause ought to refer to the *acts* of Aeschines about
which he is going to speak, not to his parentage, which the orator
has done with.

Glaucothea. Her real name is said to have been Glaucis.
Glaucothea was the name of a sea-nymph. The change of the
father's name Tromes ('Trembler') to Atrometus ('Dauntless')
would also betoken a rise in the world.

Empusa, or 'The Foul Phantom' : a female demon capable
of assuming any shape. Obscene ideas were sometimes associated
with her.

§ 132. For Antiphon, see Introd. to Speech on the Embassy.
struck off the list : at the revision of the lists in 346. (Each

deme revised the list of its own members, subject to an appeal to the courts.)

without a decree : i.e. a decree authorizing a domiciliary visit.

§ 134. *when . . . you elected him.* See Introd. to Speech on the Embassy.

from the altar : a peculiarly solemn form of voting ; it is mentioned in the Speech against Macartatus, § 14.

§ 136. *when Philip sent,* &c. See Introd. to Speech on the Embassy.

§ 137. The ostensible purpose of Anaxinus' visit was to make purchases for Olympias, Philip's wife. Aeschines states that Anaxinus had once been Demosthenes' own host at Oreus.

§ 141. *paternal deity* : as father of Ion, the legendary ancestor of the Ionians, and so of the Athenians.

§ 143. *and of one,* &c. I have followed the general consensus of recent editors ; but I do not feel at all sure that the antecedent of *is* is not πόλεμος. In that case we should translate, ' which led to Philip's coming to Elateia and being chosen commander of the Amphictyons, and which overthrew,' &c.

§ 146. *nature of the resources,* &c. : i.e. especially the possession by Athens of a strong fleet.

§ 148. *representatives on the Council.* The Amphictyonic Council was composed of two representatives (Hieromnemones) from each of twelve primitive tribes, of which the Thessalians, the Boeotians, the Ionians (one of whose members was appointed by Athens), and the Dorians (one member appointed by Sparta) were the chief, while some of the tribes were now very obscure. There were also present delegates (Pylagori) from various towns. These were not members of the Council, and had no vote, but might speak. Athens sent three such delegates to each meeting. (See Goodwin, pp. 338, 339.)

§ 150. *make the circuit,* or ' beat the bounds '. The actual proceedings (according to Aeschines' account, summarized in the Introd. to this Speech) were much more violent.

It was clearly impossible, &c. The argument is unconvincing.

Aeschines may have known of the intention of the Locrians without their having served a formal summons.

§ 158. *one man* : i. e. Philip.

§ 169. *the Prytanes* : the acting Committee of the Council.

set fire to the wicker-work : i. e. probably the hurdles, &c., o[f] which the booths were partly composed.   Probably a bonfire wa[s] a well-understood form of summons to an Assembly called in [an] emergency.

the draft-resolution.   See Introd., vol. i, p. 18.

on the hill-side : i. e. on the Pnyx, the meeting-place of [the] Assembly.

§ 171. *the Three Hundred.*   See n. on § 102.

§ 176. *philippize.*   The word was coined during the wars w[ith] Philip, on the analogy of ' medize '—the term used of the ac[ts] of the traitors who supported the invading Persians (Medes) [in] in the fifth century.

§ 177. *to Eleusis*, which was on the most convenient (th[ough] not the shortest) route for an army marching to Thebes.

§ 180. *Battalus* : a nickname given to Demosthenes by [his] nurse on account of the impediment in his speech from which he suffered in early days, or of his general delicacy.   Aeschines had tried to fix an obscene interpretation upon it.

Creon.   See Speech on the Embassy, § 247.

at Collytus : i. e. at the Rural Dionysia held in that deme.

§ 189. *any one* : lit. ' any one who chooses,' i. e. to call him to account.   The expression (ὁ βουλόμενος) is apparently half technical, as applied to a self-appointed prosecutor.   (Cf. Aristophanes, *Plutus* 908 and 918.)

§ 194. *the general* : i. e. at Chaeroneia.

§ 195. *Philip employed.*   Most editors say ' *Aeschines* employed '.   But this would require οὗτος not ἐκεῖνο , and § 218 also supports the interpretation here given.

§ 198. *treasured up*, &c.   The suggestion seems to be that Aeschines foresaw the disasters, but concealed his knowledge, ' storing them up ' in order to make a reputation out of them later.

§ 204. *to leave their land*, &c.: i.e. at the time of Xerxes' invasion in 480, when the Athenians abandoned the city and trusted to the 'wooden walls' of their ships.

§ 208. On this magnificent passage, see the treatise *On the Sublime*, chaps. xvi, xvii.

§ 209. *poring pedant*: lit. 'one who stoops over writings'. Here used perhaps with reference to Aeschines' having 'worked up' allusions to the past for the purpose of his Speech, while he remained blind to the great issues of the present. Many editors think that the reference is to his earlier occupation as a school-master or a clerk; but this is perhaps less suitable to the context.

§ 210. *staff . . . ticket*. The colour of the staff indicated the court in which the juror was to sit; the ticket was exchanged for his pay at the end of the day.

§ 214. *a very deluge*. He is thinking, no doubt, of the disaster at Chaeroneia and the destruction of Thebes.

§ 215. *while their infantry*, &c. The Theban forces when prepared for action would naturally camp outside the walls (see Olynth. I, § 27, where Demosthenes similarly thinks of the Athenian army encamping outside Athens). But although they were thus encamped outside, and had left their wives and children unguarded within, they allowed the Athenian soldiers to enter the city freely.

§ 216. *the river*: probably the Cephisus. Both battles are otherwise unknown. If one of them was in winter, it must have taken place not long after the capture of Elateia, and several months before the battle of Chaeroneia.

§ 219. *somewhere to lay the blame*: or possibly, 'some opportunity of recovering himself,' or 'some place of retreat'. But the interpretation given (which is that of Harpocration) is supported by the use of ἀνενεγκεῖν in § 224.

§ 227. *counters all disappear*. The calculation was made by taking away, for each item of debt or expenditure, so many counters from the total representing the sum originally possessed. When the frame (or *abacus*) containing the counters was left clear, it meant that there was no surplus. (The right reading, however, may be ἂν καθαιρῶσιν, 'if the counters are decisive,' or ἂν καθαιρῶσιν, 'whatever the counters prove, you concede.')

§ 231. *cancel them out* (ἀντανελεῖν): strictly, to strike each out of the account in view of something on the opposite side (i. e. in view of the alternative which you would have proposed).

§ 234. *collected in advance*: i. e. Athens had been anticipating her income.

§ 238. *if you refer*, &c. Aeschines had accused Demosthenes of saddling Athens with two-thirds of the expense of the war, and Thebes with only one-third.

three hundred, &c. See Speech on Naval Boards, § 29 n.

§ 243. *customary offerings*, made at the tomb on the third and ninth days after the death.

§ 249. *Philocrates*: not Philocrates of Hagnus, the proposer of the Peace of 346, but an Eleusinian. For Diondas, see § 222. The others are unknown.

§ 251. *Cephalus.* Cf. § 219. He was an orator and statesman of the early part of the fourth century. (The best account of him is in Beloch, *Attische Politik*, p. 117.)

§ 258. *the attendants' room.* The 'attendants' are those who escorted the boys to and from school—generally slaves.

§ 259. *the books*, &c. Cf. § 129 and notes. The books probably contained the formulae of initiation, or the hymns which were chanted by some Dionysiac societies. The service described here is probably that of the combined worship of Dionysus-Sabazios and the Great Mother (Cybele).

dressing, &c. The candidate for initiation was clothed in a fawn-skin, and was 'purified' by being smeared with clay (while sitting down, with head covered) and rubbed clean with bran, and after the initiation was supposed to enter upon a new and higher life. It is possible that the veiling and disguising with clay originally signified a death to the old life, such as is the ruling idea in many initiations of a primitive type. (Cf. Aristophanes, travesty of an initiation-ceremony in the *Clouds* 256.)

§ 260. *fennel and white poplar.* These were credited with magical and protective properties.

Euoe, Saboe : the cry to Sabazios. One is tempted to render it by ' Glory ! Hallelujah ! ' In fact, the Dionysiac ' thiasoi ', or some of them, had many features, good as well as bad, in common with the Salvation Army. The cry ' Euoe, Saboe ' is of Thracian origin ; ' Hyes Attes ' is Phrygian. The serpents, the ivy, and the winnowing-fan figured in more than one variety of Dionysiac service. It is not certain that for ' ivy-bearer ' (κιττοφόρος) we should not read ' chest-bearer ' (κιστοφόρος) used with reference to the receptacle containing sacred objects, of which we hear else-where in connexion with similar rites.

§ 261. *fellow-parishioners :* lit. ' members of your deme '. Each deme kept the register of citizens belonging to it. Enrol-ment was possible at the age of 18 years, and had to be confirmed by the Council. (See Aristotle, *Constitution of Athens*, chap. xlii.)

§ 262. *collecting figs*, &c. Two interpretations are possible : (1) that the spectators in derision threw fruit—probably not of the best—at Aeschines on the stage, and he gathered it up, as a fruiterer collects fruit from various growers, and lived on it ; or (2) that while he was a strolling player, Aeschines used to rob orchards. Of these (1) seems by far the better in the context.

§ 267. *I leave the abysm*, &c. The opening of Euripides' *Hecuba*. The line next quoted is unknown. ' Evil in evil wise ' (κακὸν κακῶς) is found in a line of Lynceus, a fourth-century tragedian.

§ 282. *denied this intimacy with him :* or possibly (with the scholiast), ' declined this office.'

§ 284. *the tambourine-player.* Such instruments were used in orgiastic rites.

§ 285. Hegemon and Pythocles were members of the Mace-donian party, who were put to death in 317 by order of the Assembly. (See Speech on Embassy, §§ 215, 314.)

§ 287. *same libation :* i.e. the same banquet. The libation preceded the drinking. To ' go beneath the same roof ' with a polluted person was supposed to involve contamination.

in the revel. Cf. Speech on the Embassy, § 128. The reference, however, is here more particularly to Philip's revels after the battle of Chaeroneia, in which, Demosthenes suggests, the Athenian envoys took part.

§ 289. The genuineness of the epitaph is doubtful. Line 2 is singularly untrue. The text is almost certainly corrupt in places (e. g. ll. 3 and 10).

their lives, &c. As the text stands, ἀρετῆς and δείματος must be governed by βραβῆ, 'made Hades the judge of their valour or their cowardice.' But this leaves οὐκ ἐσάωσαν ψυχάς as a quasi-parenthesis, very difficult to accept in so simple and at the same time so finished a form of composition as the epigram. There are many emendations.

'Tis God's, &c. The line, μηδὲν ἁμαρτεῖν ἐστι θεῶν καὶ πάντα κατορθοῦν, is taken from Simonides' epitaph on the heroes of Marathon. The sense of the couplet is plain from § 290; but ἐν βιοτῇ in l. 10 is possibly corrupt.

§ 300. *the confederacy*, i. e. Athens, Thebes, and their allies at Chaeroneia.

§ 301. *our neighbours*, especially Megara and Corinth.

§ 308. *the inactivity which you*, &c. : i. e. abstention from taking a prominent part in public life.

§ 309. *opening of ports* ; i. e. to Athenian commerce.

§ 311. *What pecuniary assistance*, &c. Demosthenes is thinking of his own services in ransoming prisoners, &c. Some editors translate, 'What public financial aid have you ever given to rich or poor ?' i. e. 'When have you ever dispensed State funds in such a way as to benefit any one ?' It is impossible to decide with certainty between the two alternatives ; but the meanings of πολιτική (' citizen-like ', 'such as one would expect from a good fellow-citizen ') and κοινή, which I assume, seem to be supported by §§ 13 and 268 respectively.

§ 312. *leaders of the Naval Boards.* See Introd. to Speech on Naval Boards.

damaging attack, &c. This probably refers to modifications

introduced on Aeschines' proposal into Demosthenes' Trierarchic
Law of 340, not at the time of its enactment, but after some
experience of its working. (See Aeschines, ' Against Ctesiphon,'
§ 222.)

§ 313. Theocrines was a tragic actor, who was attacked in
the pseudo-Demosthenic Speech ' Against Theocrines '. Harpocration's description of him as a ' sycophant ', or dishonest
informer, may be merely an inference from the Speech.

§ 318. *your brother*. See Speech on the Embassy, §§ 237, 249.
It is not known which brother is here referred to.

§ 319. Philammon was a recent Olympic victor in the boxing
match ; Glaucus, a celebrated boxer early in the fifth century.

§ 320. *owner of a stud*. To keep horses was a sign of great
wealth in Athens.

INDEX

Oxford: Horace Hart, M.A., Printer to the University.

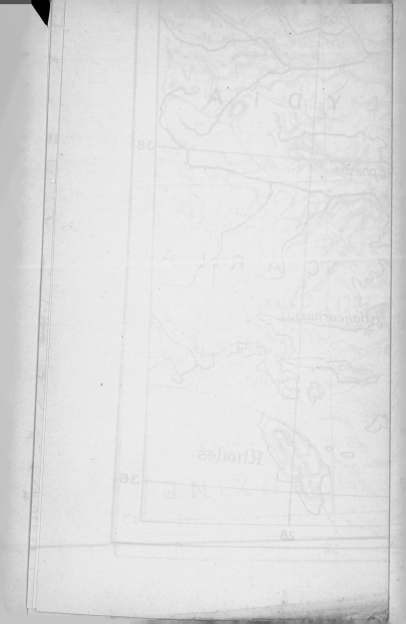

Leucas

Cephalonia

MACEDONIA

Extent of Accession of Philip
And later during first reign

Date Due